PAIN perplexity and Promotion

A Prophetic Interpretation of the Book of Job

BOB SORGE

Foreword by Joy Dawson

Seventh Printing (2015)

PAIN, PERPLEXITY AND PROMOTION: A prophetic interpretation of the book of Job

For information on all Bob's books, see page 179.

www.oasishouse.com
twitter.com/BOBSORGE
Facebook.com/BobSorgeMinistry
Blog: bobsorge.com
On Youtube, visit "Bob Sorge Channel"

Edited by Edie Veach.

Printed in the United States of America
ISBN-10: 0-9621185-6-7
ISBN-13: 978-0-9621185-6-2

Library of Congress Cataloging-in-Publication Data

Sorge, Bob
     Pain, Perplexity & Promotion: A Prophetic Interpretation of the Book of Job by Bob Sorge.
     p. cm.
     Includes bibliographical references.
     1. Bible, O.T. Job Commentaries, I. Title, II. Title: Pain, Perplexity, and Promotion
     BS1415.3 .S59 1999
     233' .107--dc21

                                                            99-30852

Contents

Foreword

God has done it again—given us another "classic" through my dear friend Bob Sorge. The first was his book on *The Fire Of Delayed Answers*, and now this one.

Only a person who has been in the furnace of God's testings to the degree and length of time that Bob has, and has responded to God in the way he has, could be entrusted by God with such profound insights on the book of Job.

Do yourself a favor and pour over its contents with an open mind and a humble, hungry heart to learn what God is saying to His people at this time. I guarantee you'll finish up with a greater revelation of God's character and ways in relation to the purposes of fiery trials as they come to all who have cried out "that I may know Him and the power of His resurrection, and the fellowship of His sufferings, being conformed to His death" (Philippians 3:10).

This book is not for casual inquirers of truth, but for those who want truth at any price, and are willing to change their former theories, philosophies and theology if necessary.

— Joy Dawson

Preface

The book of Job is for today. It is a prophetic picture foretelling the nature of God's dealings in His people in the end times.

This book is not written in order to give you greater insight into a book of the Bible. It is written to enable you to understand the nature and purpose of the fire that is touching your life in these last days.

God designed that the first book of the Bible ever written should instruct and serve the saints at the very end of the ages, for there is a falling and refining that is prophesied concerning the endtime saints: *"And some of those of understanding shall fall, to refine them, purify them, and make them white, until the time of the end; because it is still for the appointed time"* (Daniel 11:35).

I am dedicating this book to today's endtime generation —the generation of my children Joel, Katie, and Michael— those who will encounter greater fires than their predecessors. I pray that this book will enlighten you as you seek to interpret the crucible and will empower you to cooperate with God's accelerated purposes in the last hour.

Read this book with understanding, as you are being refined and purified, for this is the appointed time.

Bob Sorge
Kansas City, Missouri
April, 1999

1

God Picks A Fight

If you've not done so recently, please read the first two chapters of Job. They paint the backdrop for the rest of the book. Here's the essence of the story.

Job is a godly, wealthy man with ten children who love to party. Fearing for their spiritual condition, Job regularly offers burnt offerings on their behalf to atone for their sins.

Noticing Job's piety, God says to Satan, **"Have you considered My servant Job, that there is none like him on the earth, a blameless and upright man, one who fears God and shuns evil?"**(1:8).[1] Basically, God is picking a fight with Satan, and Job is the scapegoat. And at the time this is happening, Job knows nothing of this heavenly exchange.

It is essential to highlight this truth: *the entire saga that is about to unfold is the result of God's initiation, not Satan's.* From start to finish this whole thing is God's idea.

A Divine Wager

Satan responds to God's pointing to Job in so many words: "Little wonder that Job serves You. He's no fool. You bless him; You protect him; You answer his prayers. He'd be a fool to forsake this handy arrangement he has with

---

[1] All quotations from the book of Job are printed in bold lettering.

1

You. But don't think for a moment, God, that Job serves You because He loves You. He doesn't love You for who You are; he loves You for what You do for him. He loves You only because of the blessings You lavish upon him. And if You'll give me a chance, I'll prove that to You. Take away Your hedge of protection from his life, and let me have a shot at him, and I bet he'll curse You to Your face!"

God then responds by basically saying, "You've got a deal! Go ahead, take a whack at Job; I'll remove My hedge of protection around his life. And We'll see if you're right. You can touch anything he possesses, but you must not touch his person."

So God and Satan have taken bets, and Job is the guinea pig.

Round One: Satan Touches Job's Stuff

> Now there was a day when his sons and daughters were eating and drinking wine in their oldest brother's house; and a messenger came to Job and said, "The oxen were plowing and the donkeys feeding beside them, when the Sabeans raided them and took them away—indeed they have killed the servants with the edge of the sword; and I alone have escaped to tell you!" While he was still speaking, another also came and said, "The fire of God fell from heaven and burned up the sheep and the servants, and consumed them; and I alone have escaped to tell you!" While he was still speaking, another also came and said, "The Chaldeans formed three bands, raided the camels and took them away, yes, and killed the servants with the edge of the sword; and I alone have escaped to tell you!" While he was still speaking, another also came and said, "Your sons and daughters were eating and drinking wine in their oldest brother's house, and suddenly a great wind came from across the wilderness and struck the

four corners of the house, and it fell on the young people, and they are dead; and I alone have escaped to tell you!" (1:13-19).

In the above passage, Satan killed Job's servants, took his oxen, his donkeys, his sheep, his camels, and then killed his ten children. But Job's response in 1:20-22 is absolutely incredible! He tears his robe, shaves his head, and falls to the ground in worship before God. He does not curse God as Satan had wagered. Instead, he worships!

Then Job arose, tore his robe, and shaved his head; and he fell to the ground and worshiped. And he said: "Naked I came from my mother's womb, and naked shall I return there. The LORD gave, and the LORD has taken away; blessed be the name of the LORD." In all this Job did not sin nor charge God with wrong (1:20-22).

Verse 22 affirms that Job did not sin in round one, so we go to round two.

Round Two: Satan Touches Job's Health

God also initiates the next interchange with Satan:

Then the LORD said to Satan, "Have you considered My servant Job, that there is none like him on the earth, a blameless and upright man, one who fears God and shuns evil? And still he holds fast to his integrity, although you incited Me against him, to destroy him without cause." So Satan answered the LORD and said, "Skin for skin! Yes, all that a man has he will give for his life. But stretch out Your hand now, and touch his bone and his flesh, and he will surely curse You to Your face!" And the LORD said to Satan, "Behold, he is in your hand, but spare his life." So

Satan went out from the presence of the LORD, and struck Job with painful boils from the sole of his foot to the crown of his head (2:3-7).

When God mentions Job to Satan the second time, Satan refuses to admit that he's lost the bet, so he basically says, "There's nothing more important to a man than his health. Remove Your protection from his health and You'll find out what Job really thinks about You. Because he doesn't love You for who You are, he loves You for how You bless him. Touch his health, and he'll curse You to Your face!"

So God said to Satan, "Deal! You can touch Job's body, you just can't take his life."

Each time God establishes the boundaries that Satan cannot cross. Yet Satan is masterful at inflicting pain (a truth that is embodied in the cross). He finds a way to produce maximum distress in Job's body without killing him.

How does Job respond to all this?

And he took for himself a potsherd with which to scrape himself while he sat in the midst of the ashes. Then his wife said to him, "Do you still hold fast to your integrity? Curse God and die!" But he said to her, "You speak as one of the foolish women speaks. Shall we indeed accept good from God, and shall we not accept adversity?" In all this Job did not sin with his lips (2:8-10).

Then, Job's three friends pay him a visit—to mourn with him and comfort him. They are so distraught at his deplorable condition that they sit on the ground with him for seven days and seven nights, speechless.

After seven days of silence, Job opens his mouth and vents his agony. This starts a series of dialogues between Job and his three friends, and these exchanges comprise the majority of the book (chapters 3-31). Next, a young man by the name of Elihu expounds his opinions in chapters 32-37, and then in chapters 38-41 God speaks to Job. Finally, chapter 42 tells the story of Job's restoration and subsequent bliss.

So the book starts with God picking a fight, and it ends with Satan losing his wager. Not only does Job prove that he loves God from a pure motive, but he is also radically transformed in the process. It is this transformation of Job which is the central theme of all that you are about to read. Now, let's look at the keys which unlock this book.

2

A Blameless Man

There was a man in the land of Uz, whose name was Job; and that man was blameless and upright, and one who feared God and shunned evil (1:1).

The First Key To Understanding The Book

The book of Job will never open to you until you establish this fundamental premise beyond all question: Job was a godly, blameless man who did nothing sinful to deserve the calamity that hit his life. As long as you look for things Job might have done wrong to suffer as he did, you will never unlock the mystery of this book. The consistent testimony of God in both the first and last chapters is that Job was a righteous man who maintained his piety through the greatest trial of his life.

One of the common mistakes many interpreters make is they start to search Job's life for reasons why such devastation came upon him. For example, I've heard people say that this calamity came upon him because of fear in his life. They base this on Job's statement in 3:25, **"For the thing I greatly feared has come upon me, and what I dreaded has happened to me."** There is a measure of truth in the teaching that we bind ourselves to that which we fear, but that's not what's going on with Job. What he feared was the destiny of his children. He knew that through his sacrificial offerings God would forgive his children, but he feared that they still might reap the consequences of their compromise and carelessness. Their deaths now seemed to confirm the validity of his fears. He did not fear for himself, but rather he had a godly fear for the welfare of his children—something which any upright parent carries. This was a healthy fear, not a misguided fear that precipitated Job's trials.

Job's calamity was not the result of fear or unbelief or pride in his life. The calamity was a result of his godliness.

The book is very clear in documenting Job's blamelessness. God Himself witnesses to Job's integrity:

- 1:8 **Then the LORD said to Satan, "Have you considered My servant Job, that there is none like him on the earth, a blameless and upright man, one who fears God and shuns evil?"**
- 2:3 **Then the LORD said to Satan, "Have you considered My servant Job, that there is none like him on the earth, a blameless and upright man, one who fears God and shuns evil? And still he holds fast to his integrity, although you incited Me against him, to destroy him without cause."**

In this latter verse, God Himself declares that there was no wicked cause for Job's distress.

The Holy Spirit further witnesses to Job's godly stature in two other portions of Scripture. In Ezekiel 14:14, Job is ranked in the same spiritual category as Noah and Daniel: "Even if these three men, Noah, Daniel, and Job, were in it, they would deliver only themselves by their righteousness,' says the Lord GOD." And James 5:11 places Job before us as a godly example of perseverance. So the Holy Spirit uses two other witnesses, Ezekiel and James (for "by the mouth of two or three witnesses every word shall be established"), to confirm Job's godliness.

Job suffered, not because of what he did wrong, but because of what he did right. Had it not been for his righteousness, God would have never bragged on him to Satan in the first place (see 1:8). It was his uncommon holiness that precipitated his trials.

This book, then, serves as a pattern to show us how God uses painful circumstances in the lives of His chosen ones—who have qualified for spiritual advancement because of their obedience and blamelessness—in order to bring them to a higher dimension of spiritual reality. Job is one of the great men of history to which Hebrews 12:23 refers when it talks about "the spirits of just men made perfect." Job was a just man whose faith and love were perfected through suffering.

Defining Blamelessness

When it says Job was blameless, it does not mean he was sinless. None of us are without sin (1 John 1:8). To be blameless is to live our lives before others so that they cannot accuse us of obvious or visible sin (1 Timothy 3:2; 6:14). Even those who are blameless before people have inner shortfalls that God sees. Those hidden sins of the heart are called iniquities, and Job recognizes he has iniquity (10:6, 14). So when he defends his integrity, he's not claiming sinlessness; he's simply claiming that there is no big black sin in his life to account for his calamity.

Sometimes we suffer pain because of sinfulness, mistakes, weaknesses, or shortcomings in our lives. But Job is a prime example that it's also possible for God's people to suffer greatly even though they've done nothing wrong. *We must recover the understanding that it's possible to do everything right and still experience great distress and upheaval. "Many are the afflictions of the righteous"* (Psalm 34:19).

It must be settled without discussion or argument: Job did nothing sinful to incur his evil calamity. The more I study this book, the higher my estimation of Job grows. He was one of the godliest men of all human history.

Job is *the* godly man of the book. I must resist any interpretation which seeks to place any other people in the book on Job's spiritual playing field. Some interpreters see Elihu as appointed by God to rebuke Job or as commissioned by God to prepare Job for his revelation of God. I disagree.

This is a book of an incredibly godly man who is surrounded by dogs, "bulls of Bashan" who run at him and gore him (Psalm 22:12). Never again does Scripture give even mention of Eliphaz or Elihu, or any of them. But what honor is given to Job in Scripture! James testifies of him: "Indeed we count them blessed who endure. You have heard of the perseverance of Job and seen the end intended by the Lord—that the Lord is very compassionate and merciful" (James 5:11). In context, James calls Job a prophet. Job is *the* man; the others do not approach Job's godliness.

The message of this book begins to unlock to us when we establish that the most dreadful calamity came upon the most righteous man on the earth. In this way and others, Job is a clear prophetic type of Christ Himself.

Needing Correction

God's opinion of Job towards the end of the book appears to be contradictory. God seems to be talking out of two sides of His mouth with the following statements:

- **"Who is this who darkens counsel by words without knowledge?"** (38:2).
- **And so it was, after the LORD had spoken these words to Job, that the LORD said to Eliphaz the Temanite, "My wrath is aroused against you and your two friends, for you have not spoken of Me what is right, as My servant Job has"** (42:7).

So which is it, Lord? Did Job darken Your counsel, or did he speak rightly of You? The answer is seen in the one to whom God is talking. *To the man's face, God speaks correction; but in speaking of him to others, God vindicates him as a devout servant who has come to understand the greater mysteries of godliness.*

Yes, Job needed correction. We all do. None of us will ever mature beyond the need for correction. But God didn't allow Job's calamities because He needed to reprimand him—He allowed them because He had a particularly wonderful dimension of spiritual leadership in Job's destiny.

The book of Job speaks directly to those saints who have kept their hearts pure before God but even so have encountered inexplicable trauma and crisis.

Walk with me, please, through this brief book. I will be as concise as possible, and show how Job serves as a pattern for the believer's life—a pattern for how God brings us into new realms of spiritual promotion. But first, let's be sure we're looking at the book from the right perspective.

3

Interpreting The Book

"**H**ermeneutics" is a fancy word Bible students use to denote "the science of interpreting the Bible." Every time we study a portion of Scripture, we are trying to interpret what it means. Hermeneutical principles, properly applied, can help us unlock the fuller meanings of God's Word.

To understand the book of Job, it is essential that we interpret correctly what is going on in the book. If we apply the right hermeneutical principles the book will come into focus. Through years of focused meditation in this book and application of such principles, I have discovered keys that have opened my understanding of the book. These hermeneutical determinations were not chosen arbitrarily nor were they gleaned from other authors, but they were uncovered one at a time—through intense identification with Job's pain and through an impassioned pursuit of the heart of God. It is this interpretation of Job that has brought great hope and expectation to my own heart in the midst of great personal calamity, and I trust it will minister the life of God to many others who need a grid or backdrop to interpret the purposes of God in their own crucible. I call this my "hermeneutical lens." It's the lens through which I view the book, based upon certain biases that I have come to embrace after careful study.

If the lens through which you view the book of Job is awry, your interpretation of the book will be skewed. If your lens is accurate, it will bring the book into crystal clarity. I submit my hermeneutical interpretation for you to judge for yourself whether my lens is accurate.

My Hermeneutical Lens

I see everything in the book of Job through the following hermeneutical determinations which will be discussed in detail throughout this book—this is my "hermeneutical lens":

1. Job is a godly and blameless man. Period.
2. His inexplicable calamity is the result of God's pleasure in his life.
3. The book is a primer on spiritual warfare, charting the perplexing territory between God's sovereign purposes, Satan's harassments, and people's opinions.
4. The purpose of the calamity is to glorify God by changing Job and bringing him to a higher spiritual inheritance.
5. The sufferings of Job parallel Christ's cross in many ways.
6. Job's journey lays a pattern for God's dealings in our lives.
7. The book is a prophecy foretelling the nature of God's dealings in preparing the church for the endtime harvest.

The Law Of First Mention

One of the most fundamental of all hermeneutical principles is what is commonly termed "the law of first mention." This principle affirms that when something is mentioned for the first time in Scripture, it carries its own unique significance. When a word or concept is first mentioned in the Bible, that word or concept (viewed in the context of its surrounding verses) provides a platform for understanding every other occurrence of that word or concept throughout the rest of Scripture. When something occurs for the first time in Scripture, the wise student will take particular note.

"The law of first mention" has particular relevance for the book of Job because it is arguably the first book of the Bible actually put on paper. While there is no way to prove beyond all doubt which Bible book was actually written first, many conservative scholars agree that the evidence points to Job. Even many of the Hebrew rabbis placed Job as the first book of their Old Testament Scriptures to be written, conjecturing that Moses learned Job's story from Job's descendants in Midian, and put the story onto paper during his forty years in the Midianite wilderness.

There is considerable controversy as to who might have authored the book—whether Job himself, or Moses, or someone else. But regardless of who authored the book, there are solid reasons for believing it to be the first book of the canon to be recorded.[1]

---

[1] Some Sources That Agree Job Was The First Bible Book Written

Matthew Henry is inclined toward ascribing the authorship of the book to Elihu, although he also admits that Job and Moses are possibilities (Matthew Henry's Commentary on the Whole Bible, Volume III, p.1).

Matthew Poole determines it is "most probable" that the author was either Job himself, or Elihu, or Moses (Matthew Poole's Commentary on the Holy Bible, Volume I, p. 921).

Kevin Conner and Ken Malmin, in their booklet "Old Testament Survey," concur that the book was probably written by Job himself.

Albert Barnes devotes fourteen pages of discussion to the issue of who authored the book of Job (Barnes' Notes, Job, pp. xiv-xxvii). After discussing the arguments for and against all the various opinions that scholars espouse, he concludes, "The considerations suggested are such as seem to me to leave no rational doubt that the work was composed before the departure from Egypt" (p. xxiv). Barnes believes that all the objections are best answered in ascribing the authorship to Job himself (with slight modifications from someone subsequently, such as the mention of Job's death). He puts forward these reasons: (1) Job had ample time to record his trials during the 140 years he lived after his calamity; (2) Since Job understood the art of writing books, 19:23-24, "and having abundant leisure, it is scarcely to be conceived, that he would have failed to make a record of what had occurred during his own remarkable trials." I will add to this my own personal observation that most saints who go through great calamities are inclined to write or journal their experiences; (3) It is highly unlikely to suppose after Job had experienced something that would furnish such important lessons to mankind, that he would entrust the recollection of it all to the uncertainty of spoken tradition; (4) "Job has shown in his own speeches that he was abundantly able to compose the book" (p. xxvi). *(Continued on next page)*

Many of the great saints of early times are said to have been devoted to the study of two Bible books in particular: Job and Revelation. That's not surprising, as these are the bookends of the Bible, reflecting between each other the ways of God. We use the expression "from Genesis to Revelation," but we might just as easily say "from Job to Revelation." Since the book of Genesis occurs first chronologically in the canon, many of us have assumed that it was the first Bible book written. If you've assumed (like I always had) that Genesis was the first Bible book written, I hope you can open your thinking to the possibility that Job was written before Moses wrote Genesis.

I will take the remainder of this chapter to validate my claim that Job is the first Bible book written, because I draw some very important conclusions based upon that premise. I believe it is of critical significance in the purposes of God that Job was the first Bible book put on paper, so I will lay out the factors which suggest an early date for the book.

Validating An Early Date For Job

Here are five reasons why I favor an early date for Job:

1. **Job's function as priest of his family places him in the patriarchal period.**

The book opens with Job sacrificing burnt offerings on behalf of his children. The patriarchs Abraham, Isaac,

---

(Continued from previous page) Thus, after a substantial discussion of the case, Albert Barnes concludes: "It seems to me, therefore, that by this train of remarks, we are conducted to a conclusion attended with as much certainty as can be hoped for in the nature of the case, that the work was composed by Job himself in the period of rest and prosperity which succeeded his trials, and came to the knowledge of Moses during his residence in Arabia, and was adopted by him to represent to the Hebrews, in their trials, the duty of submission to the will of God, and to furnish the assurance that he would yet appear to crown with abundant blessings his own people, however much they might be afflicted" (p. xxvii).

So whether the authorship is ascribed to Moses, Elihu, or Job, all these scholars concur that the book of Job was written before Moses wrote the book of Genesis.

and Jacob all erected altars of sacrifice to God. But that practice changed dramatically at Mt. Sinai when God gave the law and inaugurated Aaron as high priest over God's people. From that point on, God accepted burnt offerings only through the Levitical priesthood. Therefore, it's clear that Job lived before the time of Moses and Aaron—in the era of the patriarchs (the era in which the father served as priest of the household).

2. There is no mention in Job of God's dealings with the people of Israel.

Job is clearly a Gentile, but even if he lived during the early days of the people of Israel, one would expect to have some sort of reference to God's dealings with His covenant people. Nothing in the book points to the God who parted the Red Sea; everything in the book points to the God who created the heavens and the earth. The fact that Job appears to ignore Abraham, Isaac, and Jacob would suggest that he himself pre-dated them.

If the book of Job were written after the time of Moses, we would expect some hint in the book that the author was aware of the ten plagues in Egypt, the Red Sea crossing, and all the glorious power of God demonstrated at the release of His people from Egypt. The fact that the author seems oblivious to these high water marks of God's power would suggest that the book was written before Moses—and thus written before Genesis (which Moses wrote).

3. God calls Job the most eminently righteous man on the globe (1:8), which would suggest that Abraham and Melchizedek had not yet come into their own.

God testified to Satan that Job was absolutely unparalleled in spiritual stature among all the inhabitants of the earth. Considering the spiritual stature of Abraham, Isaac, Jacob, and Joseph, it's difficult to suppose that God would compare them to Job in such a diminutive way as to say,

"there is none like him on the earth" (1:8). Surely no one would argue that the patriarchs were in many respects "like" Job in character and integrity. So for God to say this about Job, Job must have lived before the patriarchs.

The Bible says that Melchizedek was even greater than Abraham, for Abraham tithed to Melchizedek, and Melchizedek in turn blessed Abraham. Hebrews 7:7 affirms that the lesser is blessed by the greater, thus making Melchizedek greater than Abraham. So the tenor of God's statement in Job 1:8 would suggest that Job lived before Melchizedek and the patriarchs.

Furthermore, prior to Abraham there were several centuries when no outstanding saints were mentioned. Genesis 10-11 doesn't commend a single person in the centuries between Noah and Abraham for his godliness, but it does point to the growing wickedness of mankind during that period. If Job lived during those dark years, God's statement in Job 1:8 makes all the more sense: **"there is none like him on the earth."**

4. Job appears to have lived longer than Abraham, validating a pre-Abrahamic date.

To substantiate this fourth point I will have to get a little intricate with arithmetic, so please stay with me.

Before the flood, men lived for a long time, many of them living for over 900 years. After the flood, people began to live increasingly shortened life spans. We don't know exactly what caused this to happen, but Genesis 11 documents how men's life spans steadily decreased.

- Noah lived 950 years (Genesis 9:29).
- Shem, his son, lived only 600 years (Genesis 11:10-11).
- Arphaxad (Shem's son) lived 438 years (Genesis 11:12-13).
- Peleg (Arphaxad's great-grandson) lived 239 years (Genesis 11:18-19).

- Abraham lived 175 years (Genesis 25:7).
- Jacob lived 147 years (Genesis 47:28).
- Joseph lived 110 years (Genesis 50:26).

Therefore, during this period, one's life span became a solid indicator of when that person lived chronologically on the time line of ancient history. For example, if Job lived 175 years or less, we could reasonably assume that he lived during or after Abraham. If Job lived longer than 175 years, we could reasonably assume that he lived before Abraham.

So the question is, how long did Job live?? If we know how long he lived, we know how to date him in relation to Abraham. But the Bible doesn't tell us how long Job lived. It does tell us, however, that he lived 140 years after his trial (Job 42:16). But how old was he at his trial? If we knew that, simple arithmetic would tell us his life span. There are some elements that help us to "guess" at how old Job might have been during the season of his personal calamity.

First of all, based upon Genesis 11:12-24, it's reasonable to suppose that Job began having children at age 30 or later.

Secondly, at the time of his calamity Job's children were already grown and living in their own houses, having each other over for parties. Since he had ten grown children, we would have to put Job's oldest child at age 40 or older. (Job 19:17 suggests that Job had grandchildren, which would mean his children would have to be in childbearing years.)

Thirdly, Job's three friends—who are obviously his contemporaries in age—are described by Elihu as being **"very old"** (32:6). So Job was already "very old" at the time of his calamity, a term which one would expect to be applied to someone who would be at least 100 years old or more.

But even if we're conservative and say that Job was only 70 at his calamity, 70 plus 140 would still add up to 210 years total life span. And again, I think this number is conservative. The Septuagint says, "And all the years that Job lived were two hundred and forty."[2]

---

[2] Clarke's Commentary, Volume III, p. 194.

So if Job lived 210 years or longer, let's now place him on the time line of Genesis 11. It's clear that he must have lived before Abraham.

Now to my fifth and final reason for giving Job an early date:

5. As Gentiles, Job and his friends walked in a level of revelation that was not generally available to Gentiles after God's covenant with Abraham, Isaac, and Jacob.

Before Abraham, God graciously revealed Himself at a certain level universally to men of all nations. Noah was a Gentile like everyone else on earth when God came to him; Enoch was a Gentile who walked with God; Melchizedek was a Gentile who served as a high priest before God. Even Abraham was a Gentile.

We derive the word "Jew" from "Judah," Jacob's son. So in broad terms, a Jew is a descendant of Jacob. But once God came to Abraham, Isaac, and Jacob, everything changed. God narrowed His self-revelation from a broad to a focused beam, and two things happened: the Israelites came into incredibly greater light, and the Gentiles fell into much greater darkness.

But Job did not live under that darkness. God visited Job in a day when the Gentiles were still eligible for revelation from God. This would further confirm that Job lived before Abraham, before the time when God narrowed His revelation to the covenant descendants of Abraham.

The evidence is compelling: Job lived before Abraham. Since the exodus from Egypt is not even hinted at, it seems the book was written prior to the exodus, making it the first book of the Bible put on paper.

Come with me to the next chapter as we begin to look at the significance of this premise.

4

Job The Pioneer

As the first book of the Bible written, Job becomes a pre-cedent-setting book. When the Holy Spirit prepared to in-spire Holy Scripture, He calculated very purposefully how He would direct its formation. It's not an accident or mere happenstance that the Holy Spirit started the whole thing off with Job.

Cornerstone Of Scripture

Job is an incredibly strategic book. As the first building block of all Scripture, it serves as the initial cornerstone of all inspired revelation. If the cornerstone is in place cor-rectly, the rest of the building can rise in perfect alignment and symmetry. If the cornerstone is awry, the entire build-ing will be planted on a skewed foundation and will eventu-ally crumble.

Under "the law of first mention" (discussed in Chapter Three) the entire book of Job takes on a special significance as the first Bible book written. Thus, Job is a ground-break-ing, foundation-laying, pioneering, apostolic book that be-comes the cornerstone of all theology. It is the beginning basis for our understanding of God and His ways.

If your foundation is wrong, the whole building is weak. When the Lord visited me personally with calam-ity, I felt like He took the foundation of all my theological understandings, swept them out from under my feet, tenderly watched me crash, and then He slowly began to remove the rubble and start the rebuilding process. And He said, "We're going to rebuild this whole thing on the book of Job."

A Primer On Spiritual Warfare

As the first Bible book written, the book of Job constitutes a primer on spiritual warfare, charting the perplexing territory between God's sovereign purposes, Satan's harassments, and people's opinions.

Job had the hand of God on him, the hand of Satan on him, and the hand of man on him—and he couldn't distinguish between them. He became dizzy with trying to sort through the whole tangled mess, because he couldn't really identify clearly from which direction things were hitting him.

The Job crucible is a place of great perplexity. When you're in the fire, you don't know where the heat is coming from, or why. Your head begins to swim as you're caught in the swirl of trying to discern cause and effect.

Job is apostolic in that he pioneered the whole arena of spiritual warfare. He was the first one to ever document in Scripture his woundings on the perplexing battleground of spiritual warfare. Job is in the battle of his life, warring with God's sovereign purposes, Satan's evil incitements, people's carnal reproaches, and the imperfect realities of a fallen world—all elements involved in spiritual warfare. Thus, even though Job is rarely mentioned at spiritual warfare conferences, the book of Job is a primer on spiritual warfare.

Job is sailing in uncharted waters. He is going where no man has gone before. He's drawing the first map we have of spiritual warfare's battleground. Map-makers always pay a great personal price for bearing the distinguishing honor of being the first to traverse virgin territory. The early explorers laid down maps of America literally at the price of human lives (disease, shipwreck, starvation, deprivation, hardship, etc.). As the Scriptures unfold, the map of spiritual warfare will gain greater clarity, but Job is to be honored for the toll he took in giving us the first primitive map of spiritual warfare's hazards. Forerunners always pay a price.

Job is stepping on landmines, and they're exploding in his face because no one else had ever stepped there before! To explain, I'll use the example of what he says in 19:11, **"He has also kindled His wrath against me, and He counts me as one of His enemies."** Job thought God was treating him like an enemy, but in fact God was counting Job as one of His friends! "Faithful are the wounds of a friend" (Proverbs 27:6). Job didn't realize God had wounded him in His kindness, and so Job accuses God of treating him like an enemy. This is one reason God later says to Job, **"Who is this who darkens counsel by words without knowledge?"** (38:2). Job will learn this lesson (and many others) by the time the battle is over, but he'll have triggered many landmines in the process.

So here's Job, all bloody from the latest bomb that has exploded in his face, and he hoarsely whispers to us, "Don't step there, that thing will blow your leg off." And then contemporary readers will stand back in the safety of their comfortable perch and criticize him. "Job shouldn't have spoken like that," they say. "He had a lot of bad attitudes!" In one sense that's true, but I just want to say this about Job: Give the guy a break! He had no Scriptures, no map, no prophetic word, no witness from someone else who had walked this way before. He was the first one! So rather than being critical of him, I think we should be extremely grateful for a godly man who was faithful to God through the greatest maze of perplexity that any man had ever encountered up to that point in human history.

The Most Misunderstood Book

The book of Job is one of the most misunderstood books in the Bible. Until you've lived a little bit of it, it's virtually impossible to understand it properly. I realize this book is unique from many other commentaries on Job. I would read commentaries on Job, look at their analysis, and say to myself, "This author has never lived this thing." It wasn't until I began to live through some hard things that the book of Job began to open to me.

I know some people wish Job wasn't in the Bible. Because I was once one of them. I had the experience in my early years of ministry of preparing a sermon, and being very impressed with it. "This thing slices; it dices; it pops; it sizzles." I could see it: this sermon will have Satan's hordes cowering at the gates of hell, and it will have the saints on their feet, cheering. The sermon was perfect, a well-fashioned arrow, except for one little "fly in the ointment": the book of Job. Everything else in the Bible seemed to support my beautifully crafted sermon, but the book of Job was the one book that seemed to contradict it. What about Job? Can I just preach my sermon and forget about the fact that the book of Job exists?

No I can't, not any longer. Now I see it. If it doesn't line up with the book of Job, it's got to go, because the book of Job establishes the theological framework against which all other theological understandings must be measured. If you get Job wrong, then nothing else can be fully right.

As the endtime storms hit this planet, everything that can be shaken will be shaken (Hebrews 12:27-28). *The only theological framework that will not be totally shaken in the last hour will be one that is firmly fixed in a true knowledge of the God of Job.*

So now the question becomes one of paramount importance: what is the book of Job all about?

The Book's Theme

I want to express in one broad, general sentence what I believe is happening in the book. To uncover this understanding was a very long and painful journey personally, and it carries great implications that I will articulate in the rest of this book. So here it is: *In broad strokes, the life of Job is a pattern for all believers of how God takes a blameless, godly man, with a life of personal purity and a yes in his spirit, and brings him through the fire to a higher inheritance.*

Job came out of the crucible with a life message that has spoken to God's people ever since. Here are some of the poignant truths Job's life declares:

- Sometimes God is totally perplexing.
- There are things going on in the spirit dimension that you don't see.
- If you've been walking blamelessly and faithfully before God, and something incredibly mystifying and even traumatic happens to you which seems to have no reasonable cause, then heighten your spiritual alertness—God might be in the process of bringing you into spiritual promotion.
- If you will guard your purity, increase your pursuit of God, and commit yourself to unquestioning obedience, He will eventually unfold His purposes to you.
- Realize that God loves to glorify Himself by salvaging the calamities of his saints, producing the superlative out of the impossible.

A Pattern To Get Your Bearings

Job's life message serves as a model or a pattern against which others can measure God's disciplines in their lives. When you have a grid for measuring what is happening in your life, you're able to cooperate with God's purposes. But without that grid or pattern you're very likely to partner with the accuser, cop an attitude toward God, and end up aborting the process. Without any prototype for understanding God's dealings, it's very difficult to say, "You have dealt well with Your servant, O LORD, according to Your word" (Psalm 119:65). Instead, it's easy to echo the accusation of the

Israelites, "It is useless to serve God" (Malachi 3:14). God wants us to steer clear of that pitfall so He has given us the pattern of Job.

Job, then, was a pioneer, a pathfinder, a forerunner whom God baptized into "the School of the Spirit," in order that he might serve as a living parable to all generations after him. His life serves as a compass, enabling us to get our bearings when we're under the disciplines of God.

Sometimes we think we know who God is. God says, "None of you know who I am! Unless I show you." So God devastated every understanding Job thought he had of God and began to rebuild Job's theology on the truth of Isaiah 55:9, "For as the heavens are higher than the earth, so are My ways higher than your ways." So Paul cried, "Oh, the depth of the riches both of the wisdom and knowledge of God! How unsearchable are His judgments and His ways past finding out!" (Romans 11:33).

God operates in a dimension that totally surpasses our human analysis. *And here's a signature of God's ways: He loves to redeem impossible messes.* He loves entangled imbroglios that have no human solution, that are hopeless catastrophes apart from divine intervention.

Sometimes God allows the saint to be reduced to seeming defeat, filled with anguish and reproach, with Satan gleefully savoring his upper hand. Or sometimes the saint is trapped by crushing circumstances beyond his control. When it appears that God has abandoned you, Job would cry out: "Don't quit! Trust God! It's never too late! This is the kind of situation God *loves!*"

In some situations, God steps back and says, "Too easy. If I step in now, they won't glorify My name for the answer." Thus He waits things out a bit, and lets the situation become even more critical so that there will be no question about the source when He intervenes with His sovereign deliverance. He loves to do the impossible!

Job Helped Abraham

Earlier, I emphasized the fact that Job pre-dated Abraham. Here's why: It's very likely that Job served as a forerunner for Abraham, helping Abraham interpret God's hand in his life.

God had said to Abraham, "Take now your son, your only son Isaac, whom you love, and go to the land of Moriah, and offer him there as a burnt offering on one of the mountains of which I shall tell you" (Genesis 22:2). Basically God said, "Kill your son."

But Abraham also knew what God had said to Noah, "Whoever sheds man's blood, by man his blood shall be shed" (Genesis 9:6). So Abraham faced a crossroads: "Do I follow my theology, or do I follow the voice?" In that moment of critical decision, it's very possible that Abraham thought to himself, "Job! I'm in a Job situation! God is vaporizing my theology. If I'm faithful like Job was, God will lead me to a higher place." Part of the reason Abraham was able to cooperate with God's purposes was because he had Job.

Redemption's Greatest Crossroads

In fact, I want to suggest that Job became a forerunner for the most eminent of saints, helping them navigate the greatest crisis points of redemptive history. At the crucial crossroads of God's redemptive plan, when *everything* was at stake, Job's life served as a pattern enabling them to make the right choice.

Joseph didn't realize that he stood at a vital juncture of God's purposes. Everything was in the balance. Would Joseph respond properly to his enslavement and imprisonment? If he would blow it, there would be no sovereign provision for Jacob's family during the seven years of terrible famine. Thankfully, Joseph had Job! Job provided Joseph with a grid for understanding the pain of his prison, empowering him to persevere successfully to the completion of God's purposes.

Moses also stood at a critical crossroads of God's redemptive plan. Would Moses respond properly to the shattered dreams, to the unfulfilled promises, to the seeming
abandonment by God? If he would pass the test, God would
have a man to lead His people forth from Egypt. Thankfully, Moses had Job! Job's journey became a model that enabled Moses to walk forward into God's highest and best.

David was another man at a critical crossroads. He was
anointed as king, but was running for his life from Saul.
Every promise of God seemed to be violated. If David would
respond properly in this crucible, he would emerge with
the promise of an eternal throne. If he would give up, how
could we call Jesus the Son of David? Thankfully, David
had Job! Job's example gave David the courage to persevere unto God's highest and best.

We are now facing another critical moment in God's
plan: the return of Christ. In preparation for Christ's coming, God is taking many of His servants through the Job
crucible. A fire has been kindled in the earth to awaken the
bride with passion for her Bridegroom. Will she persevere
to the end, or will she abort God's purposes? Thankfully,
she has Job!

Everybody had Job for an example, except for one
man: Job! This is why Job is so admirable. He persevered
through the crucible with no predecessor, no forerunner,
no pattern from which to gain comfort. Job had nobody.
He was charting virgin territory, going where no man had
gone before. He was making an unprecedented foray onto
the swirling battleground of spiritual warfare, where God's
purposes and Satan's incitements and people's opinions
combine to season the soul.

As a result of Job's faithfulness, God decided to use his
example to comfort every generation, providing them with
a compass to help them interpret their pathway. We enjoy
the same benefit today. Instead of aborting His purposes in
our lives, we are now able to cooperate with His grace and
enter into our highest inheritance.

5

Job The Worshiper

While he was still speaking, another also came and said, "Your sons and daughters were eating and drinking wine in their oldest brother's house, and suddenly a great wind came from across the wilderness and struck the four corners of the house, and it fell on the young people, and they are dead; and I alone have escaped to tell you!" Then Job arose, tore his robe, and shaved his head; and he fell to the ground and worshiped. And he said: "Naked I came from my mother's womb, and naked shall I return there. The LORD gave, and the LORD has taken away; blessed be the name of the LORD"(1:18-21).

This is the Bible's first mention of worship, and as such it is highly significant and foundational to our understanding of the true essence of worship. Jesus said, "for the Father is seeking such to worship Him" (John 4:23). In other words, the Father isn't seeking worship, He's seeking worshipers. What does it mean to be a worshiper?

The Test Of True Worship

You do not find out if you're a worshiper on Sunday morning. Anybody can worship in church on Sunday morning. The saints are gathered in holy convocation, the musicians hold the instruments of the Lord, the worship leader is anointed and ready with a killer songlist, and the singers are prayed up and fired up. If you can't worship in church on Sunday morning, you're a stone!

Let me tell you when you find out if you're a worshiper: when the bottom of your world caves in, and everything you've ever known begins to crumble around you, and you don't understand why everything hurts so much. What will you do now? Will you fall down before your Creator and worship? Or will you listen to the voices in your ear that accuse God, and then get angry at Him? Will you worship, or will you curse?

Job is the ultimate model of extravagant worship. When everything was taken from him, including his ten children, he fell before the Lord and worshiped.

And notice what he said: **"The LORD gave, and the LORD has taken away; blessed be the name of the LORD."** Job blessed God's name. God's name represents His character, His person, who He really is in all His glorious attributes. I once knew a dark time when I could not praise His works, nor could I give thanks for His ways. Because when I looked at His works in my life, they were utterly painful and extremely distressful. His ways seemed destructive to me (although I later saw that they were re-constructive). At that moment of darkness, I had no praise in my heart for His hand in my life. But through the force of the pain, I was able to say with Job, **"Blessed be the name of the LORD."** Now matter how hard it gets, you can always say, "Blessed be the name of the LORD."

In other words, what you're saying to the Lord is, "I know You're true. I know You're righteous. I know You're just. I know You're good. Even though it appears to me that You're not being just and good right now, I know that You are. So I praise You for who You are, I bless Your name."

True worship isn't experienced on Sunday morning in church; it's experienced on Monday morning, when you go to work with those uncircumcised Philistines. *Worship is tested in the crucible of everyday living.*

Worship And Prayer

The Father is making us worshipers in the order of Job, who respond to life's greatest heartaches by falling before our Creator and worshiping Him in spirit and in truth. Job maintains the posture of a worshiper throughout the book. As a worshiper, he lives a lifestyle of constant prayer. Worship is one expression of prayer. Job said it was the wicked person who says, **"And what profit do we have if we pray to Him?"**(21:15). It is the voice of wickedness that tries to tell us our prayers are availing nothing. Even when it seemed like God wasn't listening, Job never stopped praying.

Don't ever give up calling on God! God responds to those who set their face steadfastly toward Him and cry to Him without ceasing. Job kept giving His heart to God until the answer came.

This is Job's salvation: he kept praying. Over and again he lifted his gaze to God. Job is the only person in the book who prays. Job's friends say much about God, but nothing to Him. His friends talked *about* God, but Job talked *to* God. I wonder what would have happened if Job's friends, instead of talking to Job about God, had talked to God about Job.

God Promotes Worshipers

Job became a candidate for promotion because He worshiped God at each step in the process. First, he began as a worshiper. He possessed his own vessel in holiness and uprightness (1 Thessalonians 4:4), and offered sacrifices regularly for his family. God came to Job because he was a worshiper, and allowed the first test.

Job's response to the first test was once again worship—"Then Job arose, tore his robe, and shaved his head; and he fell to the ground and worshiped." It was Job's response of worship at this critical juncture that precipitated the greatest test of all in the following chapter (his physical affliction).

Worshipers beware. *It is dangerous to be a worshiper.* When you adopt a pattern of constantly giving your heart to God, get ready—He may just very well take it. (We do great with giving Jesus our all—until He takes it!) An extravagant worshiper who is constantly giving his entire being to God is dancing with a fire that's hotter than he realizes. Extravagant worshipers who are constantly crying out for more of Him are those who will get the answer to their prayers. They will qualify for the hotter flame.

6

Job's Wife

So Satan went out from the presence of the LORD, and struck Job with painful boils from the sole of his foot to the crown of his head. And he took for himself a potsherd with which to scrape himself while he sat in the midst of the ashes. Then his wife said to him, "Do you still hold fast to your integrity? Curse God and die!" But he said to her, "You speak as one of the foolish women speaks. Shall we indeed accept good from God, and shall we not accept adversity?" In all this Job did not sin with his lips (2:7-10).

One can certainly feel great sympathy for Job's wife for she lost as much as Job did, except for her health. She was plummeted into great grief for but one reason: she was married to Job. Job was the man that God and Satan were both after, but his wife was caught in the snare as well. Who feels the loss of children like a mother? Truly her grief was also beyond measure.

"Curse God And Die!"

And yet, the story makes clear that she didn't have the same spiritual reservoir to draw upon as Job had in this season of crisis. She had not cultivated the same spiritual depth of heart as her husband had, and when the storm hit, her foundations collapsed.

"Do you still hold fast to your integrity?" she asked Job. As the human being closest to Job, she affirmed Job's godliness and integrity. No one knew Job better, so she knew this hadn't happened to Job because of sin in his life. Since Job hadn't incurred God's judgment through sin, her conclusion was that God was unkind and unjust. Therefore, she offered her husband foolish counsel: **"Curse God and die!"**

Job did not sin with his mouth, but she did—and she began to feel shame and conviction over her unrighteous responses which contrasted so starkly with her husband's. So she incited him to sin. She was angry that Job didn't go off at the mouth like she did. His integrity was making her look bad. She basically said, "God hasn't done right by you even though you've walked in uprightness. So give up on God; curse Him and die!"

The obvious inference is that she herself had already cursed God in her heart. She had cursed God for her grief and pain, and now like Eve she tried to seduce her husband into the same compromise. She was angry at God, and she wanted her husband to join her.

This was a critical crossroads for Job's wife. If she had stood in faith before God, she would have shared not only in Job's valley but also in his mountaintop. But because she cursed God in her heart, she died. Not that she died physically, but she died spiritually. She had cursed God and died inside, and then she wanted her husband to do the same.

What did she die to? Spiritual fruitfulness. At the moment she cursed God, I believe Job's wife became spiritually barren. Before the story is over, Job is father to ten stunningly beautiful children. But not Job's wife. Let me explain.

A Second Wife?

I'm convinced Job's wife did not bear Job's second set of children. Here are my reasons:

- **"Curse God and die!"** The words themselves suggest that her womb died when she cursed God.
- Polygamy was very common in those days. For example, Abraham and Jacob had more than one wife. In fact, the number of wives one had back in those times was reflective of social status. Given Job's wealth and prominence, it's totally reasonable to suppose that Job married another wife after he was healed and restored.
- Job's wife had birthed and raised ten children who were grown and had children of their own. Since her children were all of partying age, it's reasonable to suppose that she herself had aged past her child-bearing years. It's quite possible she could be about 100 years old at this time, along with her husband. So to think that a woman of her age would turn around and produce ten more children that late in life is very difficult to construe.
- Job's second set of children was totally different from his first set. His first ten children were spiritually passive; his second set of children were striking in integrity and character. I believe one significant factor in the difference was their respective mothers. Job's first wife was very influential in the spiritual destiny of Job's first set of children; I am now suggesting that Job's second wife was also vitally responsible for helping Job raise up a second set of children who were beautiful in character and integrity.

Through spiritual carelessness and unbelief, Job's first wife missed her spiritual inheritance. The book doesn't condemn her, for she suffered great grief. But it is silent about her after chapter two; she was not a factor in Job's blessings. She forfeited what she could have had. If she had remained faithful to God and stood in spiritual solidarity with her husband, she could have shared in the spiritual promotion God gave Job. But she lost it all. She became a spectator instead of a participant. The invitation to greatness came to her, but she lacked the spiritual depth to discern and believe what God was doing in her husband's life, and she ended up giving up and cursing God.

Spiritual Barrenness

The parallels between Job's wife and David's wife, Michal, are remarkable. Michal also became barren because of her inability to stand with her husband, king David. Here's the passage where Michal became barren:

> *Now as the ark of the LORD came into the City of David, Michal, Saul's daughter, looked through a window and saw King David leaping and whirling before the LORD; and she despised him in her heart... Then David returned to bless his household. And Michal the daughter of Saul came out to meet David, and said, "How glorious was the king of Israel today, uncovering himself today in the eyes of the maids of his servants, as one of the base fellows shamelessly uncovers himself!" So David said to Michal, "It was before the LORD, who chose me instead of your father and all his house, to appoint me ruler over the people of the LORD, over Israel. Therefore I will play music before the LORD. And I will be even more undignified than this, and will be humble in my own sight. But as for the maidservants of whom you have spoken, by them I will be held in honor." Therefore Michal the daughter of Saul had no children to the day of her death (2 Samuel 6:16, 20-23).*

Like Job's wife, Michal's problem was unbelief. Job's wife didn't believe God was working a good thing in Job, and Michal also lost faith at a critical crossroads of her life.

Michal's crossroads came at the time David left her and ran for his life from Michal's father, king Saul. David was banished to the wilderness, and Michal stayed in Jerusalem. As the weeks and months went by, Michal lost faith in the anointing on David's life. She came to believe that David would never survive the wilderness and that her father Saul would eventually be successful in hunting David down and killing him. She lost faith in God's promises to David. When David entered the Job crucible (his seven years in the wilderness running for his life), Michal collapsed spiritually.

She thought to herself, "Why should I remain in widowhood here in Jerusalem, waiting for a man that's going to die anyways?" So in unbelief she married Palti (1 Samuel 25:44).

As the story unfolds, when David was crowned king of the land, he demanded that his wife Michal be returned to him (see 2 Samuel 3:13-16). This was David's way of rebuking Michal for her unbelief: "You thought God was finished with me, but now God has given me the throne of Israel, and you're going to have to come back to my household and see what you didn't believe."

But Michal's relationship with David was forever changed. She had lived with Palti for many years, and Palti was different from David. She had picked up Palti's values and priorities. She used to love David, but now she couldn't. The sabbatical with Palti forever changed how Michal would relate to David; she could not return to the simplicity of relationship she had with David beforehand. David had been changed profoundly in the wilderness, and since Michal refused to share the wilderness with David she remained unchanged. When she was reunited with David, David was no longer the same man she had married about eight years earlier. She could never adjust to the new David. And then when she saw him dancing before the

Lord, she could take no more. She had to express the cold cynicism that her unbelieving heart had developed.

And like Job's wife, Michal became barren through unbelief. She failed to believe that David in his integrity would qualify for God's blessings despite his trials, and she gave up on the process by marrying Palti. In the end, she became a barren bystander while God established David upon an eternal throne. Imagine living in the house with the king who has this awesome covenant with God, but never entering into it yourself because of unbelief! What could have been hers became Bathsheba's when Solomon (Bathsheba's son, not Michal's) became the heir to the throne. O the pricetag of unbelief!

Job's wife and Michal both illustrate this truth: *If God is taking someone close to you through the Job crucible, stand in faith and perseverance with that person.* If you succumb to unbelief, you will forfeit your share in the inheritance. But if you stand in faith, you will watch God fulfill His promises to that person, and you will come out together into the highlands of spiritual promotion and kingdom fruitfulness.

7

Job's Three Friends

Now when Job's three friends heard of all this adversity that had come upon him, each one came from his own place—Eliphaz the Temanite, Bildad the Shuhite, and Zophar the Naamathite. For they had made an appointment together to come and mourn with him, and to comfort him. And when they raised their eyes from afar, and did not recognize him, they lifted their voices and wept; and each one tore his robe and sprinkled dust on his head toward heaven. So they sat down with him on the ground seven days and seven nights, and no one spoke a word to him, for they saw that his grief was very great (2:11-13).

We've looked at the response of Job's wife—now let's look at how Job's friends responded to him.

These three men were genuine friends of Job. They had shared many life experiences, so when they saw his grief they shared personally in it. If they would have just mourned silently with Job, they would have done well. But they felt compelled to open their mouths, and that's where they began to make their mistakes.

At the end of the entire ordeal, God spoke to Eliphaz and said, **"My wrath is aroused against you and your two friends, for you have not spoken of Me what is right, as**

My servant Job has" (42:7). And yet all their counsel to Job was very scriptural. You can observe that by looking at the multitude of scriptural cross-references in the margin of your Bible, if you have a reference Bible with cross-references. Virtually all of their counsel can be substantiated with other Scriptures. They had good counsel—but for the wrong situation. They spoke truth, but it didn't apply to the situation at hand.

We need divine wisdom to know how to counsel people in God's ways. It's so easy to say the right thing to the wrong circumstances. Job's three friends blew it because they judged by what they saw rather than by what they heard. Jesus said, "As I hear, I judge" (John 5:30). The only way to judge what is going on in someone else's life is to hear directly from the Father regarding that person. If you try to analyze someone's situation according to your past experiences and knowledge, you will come out with "stock answers" and not help that person whatsoever. In fact, you could even disorient them. So once you learn about the challenges someone is facing, stop. Before you start giving them counsel, pray first. Wait upon the Lord to hear what He might speak. If He speaks, you can have something to say to that person; if He doesn't speak, keep quiet.

Job's Initial Cry

Job is the first one to break the silence in chapter 3 by cursing the day of his birth. Chapter 3 is the primal cry of a man in immeasurable pain. Job does not curse God, but he has to give vent to his pain somehow, and he does so by cursing the day he was born. This equates with the great cry of Christ on the cross, "And Jesus cried out again with a loud voice, and yielded up His spirit" (Matthew 27:50).

Job 3 has two counterparts in Scripture: Psalm 88 and Lamentations 3. Psalm 88 is unique from all other psalms in this respect: it has no sound of praise, thanksgiving, or hope in it. It starts with a cry of pain, it's filled with a cry of pain, and it ends with a cry of pain. The Holy Spirit gave us Psalm 88 to confirm that there is a valid place in God's processes where all one feels is pain, all one sees is darkness, and all one has are tears and questions. God never intended us to stay in that valley—we are to walk *through* the valley of the shadow of death—but there is a place of darkness in God that Psalm 88 validates. When you hit the bottom of the valley with a hard thunk, it's comforting to know others have gone before you.

An important question is, did Job sin by cursing the day of his birth? The evidence indicates that God did not view this as sinful, but rather as the heart cry of a man in great mental and physical agony. Jeremiah was a man who also knew much painful distress in his life, and he also cursed the day of his birth (see Jeremiah 20:14-18). And yet, while the Lord rebukes Jeremiah for other things, He doesn't rebuke Jeremiah for this. Before God, it seems to be a way to articulate one's pain without sinning.

Chapter 3 is the darkest part of the whole book. These are the words of a man who is smarting in the immediacy of his wounds. Over time the sharpness of the pain will dull somewhat, but right now he is absolutely writhing in agony and the darkness of total perplexity. Look at it:

- **"May the day perish on which I was born, and the night in which it was said, 'A male child is conceived.' May that day be darkness; may God above not seek it, nor the light shine upon it. May darkness and the shadow of death claim it; may a cloud settle on it; may the blackness of the day terrify it"** (3:3-5).
- **"Why did I not die at birth? Why did I not perish when I came from the womb? Why did the knees receive me? Or why the breasts, that I should nurse? For now I would have lain still and been quiet, I would have been asleep; then I would have been at rest"** (3:11-13).

- **"Why is light given to him who is in misery, and life to the bitter of soul, who long for death, but it does not come, and search for it more than hidden treasures; who rejoice exceedingly, and are glad when they can find the grave? Why is light given to a man whose way is hidden, and whom God has hedged in? For my sighing comes before I eat, and my groanings pour out like water. For the thing I greatly feared has come upon me, and what I dreaded has happened to me. I am not at ease, nor am I quiet; I have no rest, for trouble comes"** (3:20-26).

Job is not about to commit suicide. He fears God too much to take his life into his own hands. He will not kill himself, but he does long for God to kill him. Right now he's hurting so much that he just wishes God would take him. This intensity of pain does not stay with him, but right now that's where he's at. He longs for death (3:21), but death eludes him.

Job breaks the silence, and now his friends can't help themselves. They have to speak their mind, too.

"What About Job?"

This becomes the central issue in the book, "What is really going on with Job?" Job's three friends dialogue with him at length on this subject, presenting their opinions of what is going on. Their arguments are eloquent, philosophical, and poetically flourishing. *But at the root of all their sophistry is one basic tenet: they're convinced that Job's calamity is the direct consequence of sin in his life.*

Their counsel is, "Repent, God will heal you, and then you can resume with life as it should be."

Job has just one problem with that counsel: *he can't think of anything for which to repent!* I can imagine him saying, "Guys, I wish it were that simple. I wish I could just repent of a sin and, BOOM, get healed. But I can't think of anything I've done wrong. I've searched every part of my life, and I can't find any major stronghold of sin in my life. It's just not there." So Job responds to their accusations by saying, "This has not happened because of sin in my life. I don't know why this calamity has hit my life, but this much I know, it's not because of sin."

His friends say, "It's got to be sin! This isn't how God treats His friends. This is how God disciplines the disobedient. Search your heart again, Job, because there's something very wicked in you."

Job says to them, **"You see terror and are afraid"** (6:21). His friends had adopted a theology rooted in fear. Their fear was, "If God did this to you because He *likes* you, then maybe we're next! But we don't want to be next. So we have to come up with a theology that says God doesn't like you, that He's angry at you, and it's because of your wickedness."

But to every accusation Job insists upon his integrity. He says, **"Far be it from me that I should say you are right; till I die I will not put away my integrity from me"** (27:5). He's saying, "I testify that I have walked uprightly before God and that this calamity is not the result of sin. Even if I die in this thing, I will go to the grave affirming my integrity and uprightness." Now, some people view Job as self-vindicating and self-righteous. That's a cynical and inaccurate way to view Job. In the searing blast of his furnace, he is being gut-level honest. He's not playing games. He's calling it as straight as he sees it. He is being totally honest with the fact that he can't find anything of which he needs to repent.

If anyone is self-righteous in the book, it's Job's three friends. They sit in the smugness of their comfortable world and feel vindicated that they're not being judged like Job is. Their orientation is, "We're not the ones in this mess, Job, because we haven't done what you've done." *That's* self-righteousness.

Hidden From Understanding

One of the dynamics that happens in the Job crucible is this: *God closes the understanding of Job's friends so they are unable to exercise accurate discernment regarding what God is doing in Job's life.* Job offered this lament regarding his friends, **"For You have hidden their heart from understanding; therefore You will not exalt them"** (17:4).

Job is saying one thing; everyone else is saying the opposite. Job's friends gain fuel for their argument from each other. How could Job be right and everyone else wrong? This is very intimidating for Job; all his friends are on the other side of the line, and he's on this side of the line all by himself. It was the unanimous voice of all the elders versus Job's voice. Job had always appreciated and valued the input of his friends, but now he finds himself in the agonizing position of not being able to receive their perspective. And the flame is made hotter by the fact that they're all so very sincere.

If God puts you in the Job crucible, don't be surprised when all your friends fail you. It's part of the package. It goes with the territory, because God is excavating you in the very depths of your being. In their sincerity, they think they're serving you. But you feel forsaken by them. The very ones you were hoping would stand with you end up collapsing under the intensity and duration of the thing. That's how it was for Job, that's how it was for Jesus, and that's how it will be for many endtime servants.

Job's friends, like his wife, could have shared in a mighty victory if they had stayed faithful to Job and supported him loyally in his calamity. But they abandoned him to their own hurt. That abandonment was part of Job's crucible, a necessary ingredient purposely engineered by God. The issue for the friends was faith: would they believe that God is with this man, working in him, bringing him to a higher place? It's easy to doubt that this is God's man, or it's even easier to doubt that he's responding properly to the crucible.

Jesus said to His disciples, "All of you will be made to stumble because of Me this night, for it is written: 'I will strike the Shepherd, and the sheep will be scattered'" (Mark 14:27). Jesus wasn't talking about the masses, He was referring to the disciples—His friends—as those who would be scattered and leave Him. The issue for the disciples was faith: do you believe in this moment of crisis that Jesus is who He claims to be? All of them doubted and forsook Jesus.

Eliphaz

Eliphaz seems to be the senior fellow in the discussion, and so he is the most verbose of the three friends. He loses no time in attacking Job. He says, **"Surely you have instructed many, and you have strengthened weak hands. Your words have upheld him who was stumbling, and you have strengthened the feeble knees; but now it comes upon you, and you are weary; it touches you, and you are troubled"** (4:3-5).

Eliphaz is reproaching Job for being shallow spiritually—for lacking spiritual fortitude. Job had counseled people through hard times, but now that hard times have hit him, he collapses. From the start, Eliphaz is not merciful toward the intensity of Job's trial. Eliphaz simply doesn't understand what's happening with Job. He manifests the insensitivity of someone who has never known this level of brokenness. Job, in contrast, is going to come through this thing with a greater sensitivity and godly compassion for others who are torn with inexpressible heartache.

Eliphaz puts the thing on automatic rewind and plays back what he's seen in the past: **"Even as I have seen, those who plow iniquity and sow trouble reap the same"** (4:8). He's saying, "You're only reaping what you've sown, Job. You've sown wickedness, and now you're reaping the consequences."

Then Eliphaz moves into a mystical mode:

> **"Now a word was secretly brought to me, and
> my ear received a whisper of it. In disquieting
> thoughts from the visions of the night, when deep
> sleep falls on men, fear came upon me, and trem-
> bling, which made all my bones shake. Then a
> spirit passed before my face; the hair on my body
> stood up. It stood still, but I could not discern
> its appearance. A form was before my eyes; there
> was silence; then I heard a voice saying: 'Can a
> mortal be more righteous than God? Can a man
> be more pure than his Maker? If He puts no trust
> in His servants, if He charges His angels with er-
> ror, how much more those who dwell in houses
> of clay, whose foundation is in the dust, who are
> crushed before a moth?'"** (4:12-19).

Eliphaz is claiming that he has had an angelic visitation related to Job. This is the one "prophetic word" that
comes to Job, for Eliphaz is claiming to have a message
from heaven for Job. Now, not only is Job writhing in pain,
but he has to discern whether this "prophetic word" is accurate. Job concludes that Eliphaz has actually been seduced by a demon, but the process of discerning that is
very painful.

This is one dynamic that adds to the intensity of the
Job crucible. When you find yourself in the fire, others will
come to you with "messages from God." Some of them will
be true, some will be false, and the discerning process will
twist your soul. *The true words will feed your spirit, and the
false words will serve to increase the flame and actually accelerate God's purposes in your heart.*

Eliphaz moves in for another blow. **"I have seen the
foolish taking root, but suddenly I cursed his dwelling
place. His sons are far from safety, they are crushed in
the gate, and there is no deliverer"** (5:3-4). Eliphaz is

saying, "You have played the fool, Job, and as a result your children have been crushed to death." These are vicious words. With friends like this, who needs enemies?

Then Eliphaz shows his arrogance: **"But as for me, I would seek God, and to God I would commit my cause"** (5:8). He's saying, "If this were to happen to me, let me tell you what I would do." May the Lord deliver us of the arrogance of thinking that we would know how to handle the agony that others have had to endure in their misfortunes in this fallen world.

Now we come to one of the fascinating turns in the book. Eliphaz makes a statement that is quoted in the New Testament: **"He catches the wise in their own craftiness"** (5:13). Eliphaz is totally misapplying this truth, but nonetheless it's still a truth, and Paul quotes it in 1 Corinthians 3:19. It's possible in speaking truth to apply it to the totally wrong situation. Satan himself is a master at this (see Matthew 4:6-7).

Then Eliphaz makes a powerfully accurate declaration: **"Behold, happy is the man whom God corrects; therefore do not despise the chastening of the Almighty. For He bruises, but He binds up; He wounds, but His hands make whole. He shall deliver you in six troubles, yes, in seven no evil shall touch you"** (5:17-19). Eliphaz is 100% right—Job is being chastened by God. But here is where he's wrong: he thinks Job is being chastened because of Job's wickedness. He doesn't realize this truth: Job is being chastened by God because of his eminent godliness.

Like He came to Joseph, God is coming to Job and saying, "Congratulations, Job! You have kept your heart pure in an evil generation. You have walked in relationship with Me. You have chosen the ways of uprightness and integrity. Therefore, I'm calling you higher. I'm going to chasten you and bring you to a higher place in Me than you've ever known."

There are two ways to view God's chastening—as punishment or as promotion. *Yes, God does discipline and punish our sinfulness; but there is also a chastening which He brings into the lives of selected saints that He has chosen to promote because of their godliness and consecration.*

In his second speech, Eliphaz says, **"What do you know that we do not know? What do you understand that is not in us? Both the gray-haired and the aged are among us, much older than your father"** (15:9-10). Eliphaz is indignant with Job because Job is forsaking the collective wisdom of the elders. Eliphaz argues that the elderly have lived long enough to know God's ways. *What he doesn't realize is, when God strikes the earth with perplexity, no amount of experience is helpful.* The oldest and wisest are reduced to infant status before God when He manifests His endtime strategies. Experience, seniority, or tenure become irrelevant. When we're in this place, if we don't receive something from God, we know nothing.

In his third speech, Eliphaz sarcastically asks Job, **"Is it because of your fear of Him that He corrects you, and enters into judgment with you?"** (22:4). Ironically, the answer is yes!

Eliphaz concludes with his standard claim that Job needs to repent: **"If you return to the Almighty, you will be built up; you will remove iniquity far from your tents"** (22:23).

Bildad

Bildad is the second friend to speak. He utters what is one of the more cruel and insensitive statements in the book: **"If your sons have sinned against Him, He has cast them away for their transgression"** (8:4). What a way to comfort your friend! Bildad is saying that God destroyed Job's children because of their wickedness. Bildad reinforces Eliphaz's cruelty.

Bildad holds to the same overly-simplistic theology of his friends—that Job would be doing fine right now if he were as righteous as he claims to be: **"If you were pure and upright, surely now He would awake for you, and**

prosper your rightful dwelling place" (8:6). He doesn't understand the process.

In his second speech, Bildad sounds offended: **"Why are we counted as beasts, and regarded as stupid in your sight?"** (18:3). He is obviously angry and indignant that Job doesn't receive from them.

According to Bildad, here's what wickedness does to the wicked man: **"It devours patches of his skin"** (18:13). Since Job is sitting there with boils all over his skin, there's no mistaking Bildad's message. He is accusing Job of great wickedness. Bildad adds this regarding the wicked man, **"He has neither son nor posterity among his people"** (18:19). He is purposefully touching a very raw nerve in Job's soul—the loss of his children. *It is incredible how Job's friends are strategically aiming blows upon Job in order to extract the maximum amount of pain.*

Zophar

Zophar is the last and least wordy of Job's friends to respond to him. He opens by declaring to Job, **"Know therefore that God exacts from you less than your iniquity deserves"** (11:6). Job's sinfulness is so great, in Zophar's estimation, that God is actually being merciful in not punishing Job more. The fact that Job is suffering so and that the friends are not indicates how much more righteous they believe they are than Job. To think of oneself as more righteous than someone else is so easy to do—something that most of us have done. Consider this admonition of Scripture: "Let nothing be done through selfish ambition or conceit, but in lowliness of mind let each esteem others better than himself" (Philippians 2:3).

Zophar seems to be the most emotionally sensitive man of the three friends. He says, **"I have heard the rebuke that reproaches me, and the spirit of my understanding causes me to answer"** (20:3). The literal wording for *"rebuke"* is *"insulting correction."* Zophar feels insulted.

He takes Jobs comments very personally and responds out of his insecurities. His response is something of an overreaction. He describes the wicked as follows, obviously implicating Job:

"He swallows down riches and vomits them up again; God casts them out of his belly...He will restore that for which he labored, and will not swallow it down; from the proceeds of business He will get no enjoyment. For he has oppressed and forsaken the poor, he has violently seized a house which he did not build. Because he knows no quietness in his heart, he will not save anything he desires...The increase of his house will depart, and his goods will flow away in the day of His wrath. This is the portion from God for a wicked man, the heritage appointed to him by God" (20:15, 18-20, 28-29).

Zophar speaks as though he's being objective about the wicked, but he's describing Job so specifically that it's obvious he's pointing to Job personally as a very wicked man. These are Zophar's last words. He vents, and then clams up.

Job's three friends all agree on one point: When God's punishment visits a man, it's an indicator that that man must be very wicked.

Job claimed to be the exception to that rule, but they couldn't see it. It was the consensus versus the solitary voice. This is the pattern for the Job crucible.

8

Elihu

Now we come to one of the most controversial portions of the entire book—Elihu. Elihu announces his arrival into the story with color and splash, and he receives the widest assortment of analyses from commentators. I will present a perspective on Elihu that may not be popular with some. You're welcome to differ with me, but I invite you to consider my "take" on Elihu.

Elihu was a young man who spoke up in chapters 32-37 after Job's three friends were reduced to silence. We're not told what God thinks about Elihu, which is why opinions vary so widely. God rebukes Job's three friends, and He honors and restores Job, but He doesn't say anything about Elihu. So appraisals of Elihu run the entire gamut from wonderful to derogatory.

I like how Henry Halley describes Elihu: "Much of his speech consisted in telling them what Wonderful Things he was going to say. But, like the others, his chief wisdom was in the use of words which concealed rather than made plain his meaning. His main contention seems to have been that Suffering is intended of God to be Corrective rather than Punitive."[1]

---

[1] Halley's Bible Handbook, p. 246.

Elihu seems to make much more sense than Job's three friends, and so many readers take kindly to him. Frankly, I don't. I cannot laud Elihu. Let me explain.

What About Elihu?

For starters, Elihu had a temper problem. He was angry with Job because he justified himself even to the point of criticizing God, and he was angry at Job's three friends because they were inept at contradicting Job. Job was a godly man who was in the Spirit's school of training, and Elihu was angry with him—an inappropriate response. Elihu totally missed the point. Look at his anger:

> **So these three men ceased answering Job, because he was righteous in his own eyes. Then the wrath of Elihu, the son of Barachel the Buzite, of the family of Ram, was aroused against Job; his wrath was aroused because he justified himself rather than God. Also against his three friends his wrath was aroused, because they had found no answer, and yet had condemned Job. Now because they were years older than he, Elihu had waited to speak to Job. When Elihu saw that there was no answer in the mouth of these three men, his wrath was aroused** (32:1-5).

Four times it says his wrath was aroused. Elihu was working in the strength of his soul, and thus it was impossible for him to function in accurate spiritual discernment.

Second, Elihu is arrogant. His anger is a reflection of his arrogance. He thinks he knows what's going on in Job's life, and he thinks he knows what Job needs to do about it. He is unaware of how wrong his diagnosis really is. The problem with Elihu and Job's friends is this: they pontificate on subjects in which they have no learned life experience. They try to teach Job on suffering when they've never gone through a fraction of what he's experienced. It's almost impossible to bring balanced and complete counsel from such an untouched perspective.

It is very easy for young people to become trapped by the confidence that comes with trumpeting a just cause (32:2). There is a "righteous indignation" that seems so justified and yet ministers death instead of life.

Elihu represents the strong young man who is overly confident in the compartments of his theology and who easily castigates anyone who doesn't fit his mold. Elihu's success at spiritual warfare causes him to judge the weaknesses and failures of others. *Unbroken success will eventually lead to tyranny.*

One commentator expresses it well: "There is much that is elevating and instructive in Elihu's arguments and reflections; but the tone of the speech is harsh, disrespectful, and presumptuous, so that we feel no surprise at Job not condescending to answer it, but meeting it by a contemptuous silence."[2]

Elihu's Frustration With The Fathers

Elihu manifests what is a common syndrome in the church today: the frustration of young men toward the fathers in the faith. Elihu is upset with these men who are of his father's generation. He is disappointed with their performance and critical of their wisdom. Perhaps you can see his arrogance:

> **"Great men are not always wise, nor do the aged always understand justice. Therefore I say, 'Listen to me, I also will declare my opinion.' Indeed I waited for your words, I listened to your reasonings, while you searched out what to say. I paid close attention to you; and surely not one of you convinced Job, or answered his words—lest you**

---

[2] The Pulpit Commentary, Volume 7, Introduction To Job, p. vi.

say, 'We have found wisdom'; God will vanquish
him, not man. Now he has not directed his words
against me; so I will not answer him with your
words" (32:9-14).

Elihu is no fool. His irritation with his father's generation is exacerbated by the fact that he is incredibly bril-
liant and more talented than them. In many respects he's
probably more competent than them. He's chafing for his
turn at the helm of eldership. It's always easy for young
men to be critical of the older generation—until they find
themselves having to make those kinds of decisions and
then having to live with the consequences of their own un-
seasoned judgments.

Elihu has decided he is not going to repeat their mistakes. He's not going to beat around the bush and be ten-
tative with the issues. He decides he will not cower under
the fear of man; he will speak without respect of persons.
He says this in 32:21-22: **"Let me not, I pray, show par-
tiality to anyone; nor let me flatter any man. For I do
not know how to flatter, else my Maker would soon
take me away."**

Here's the danger: *It's possible under the banner of "I
will not be ruled by the fear of man" to blow people away
with your gun.*

Elihu's Shortfalls

Elihu is working with yet another blind spot: **"For I
am full of words; the spirit within me compels me"**
(332:18). Elihu is **"full of words,"** which is evidenced by
the length of his speech—six chapters! His many words
are part of his problem. I wonder if Solomon might have
had Elihu partly in mind when he wrote Proverbs 10:19,
"In the multitude of words sin is not lacking, but he who
restrains his lips is wise." In the multitude of his words,
Elihu sinned.

Sometimes it seems that Elihu has some outstanding insight, but then when you look at the conclusions he draws, you realize he wasn't taking it in the right direction. Here's his bottom-line analysis of Job: **"Oh, that Job were tried to the utmost, because his answers are like those of wicked men! For he adds rebellion to his sin; he claps his hands among us, and multiplies his words against God"** (34:36-37).

Elihu misses it by a mile. He shows how little he understands Job's crucible, how inexperienced he is in the disappointments of life, and he reveals his lack of compassionate regard for someone else's grief. Furthermore, he misjudges Job's heart intentions by accusing him of rebellion. In his sincerity, he ends up partnering with the accuser in condemning Job rather than serving him.

Elihu's words here are very foolish: **"Oh, that Job were tried to the utmost, because his answers are like those of wicked men!"** (34:36) What a horrid thing— to wish that anyone would be tried to the utmost for their sins! David declared, "He has not dealt with us according to our sins, nor punished us according to our iniquities" (Psalm 103:10). Thank God! Furthermore it says, "If You, LORD, should mark iniquities, O Lord, who could stand?" (Psalm 130:3). If God meted out to us according to our iniquities, all of us would be wiped out right now! He deals with us in incredible mercy! Therefore Elihu's words are very foolish, because Jesus said, "With the same measure you use, it will be measured to you" (Mark 4:24). Does Elihu wish that God do to him as he desired for Job, by trying him to the utmost for his own iniquity? He would surely be devastated!

It doesn't matter what Job says, Elihu criticizes it. So Elihu says, **"For Job has said, I am righteous, but God has taken away my justice; should I lie concerning my right? My wound is incurable, though I am without transgression"** (34:5-6). Job speaks rightly in this, but now look at Elihu's criticism: **"What man is like Job, who drinks scorn like water, who goes in company with the**

workers of iniquity, and walks with wicked men? For he has said, 'It profits a man nothing that he should delight in God'" (34:7-9). He is so jaded against Job that in that final phrase he ascribes to Job something that Job didn't even say! Here is where he takes on the role of the accuser, assaulting Job with false accusations.

Elihu is right in realizing that God's purpose in the crucible is to change Job, but he concludes that Job is not responding properly: **"Take heed, do not turn to iniquity, for you have chosen this rather than affliction"** (36:21). Elihu is saying that rather than embracing the affliction properly, Job is responding wrongly and thus is due to bring even greater condemnation upon himself. When you're not in the crucible, it's easy to look at someone in the crucible and think they're handling it wrong.

Why does Job not answer him? Because Elihu's arrogance and impudence don't deserve a response. Why does God not rebuke him? This is a frightening question, for Jesus said, "As many as I love, I rebuke" (Revelation 3:19). God's absence of rebuke for Elihu carries an ominous silence, a fearful foreboding of what God might be thinking about Elihu.

Everyone that God loves in the book gets rebuked by God, especially Job. *Here is a true principle seen in the book of Job: when God shows up, everyone gets a rebuke.*

Looking For Elihu At Calvary

In the next chapter, I will show a clear connection between Job's three friends and the three categories of people who sneered at Jesus to save Himself—the Jews, the Romans, and the robbers. I do not believe we're twisting Scripture to see representations of Christ's passion in the book of Job. Therefore, I began to look at Elihu from this perspective: if Job's three friends have their counterpart at the crucifixion, who is Elihu's counterpart at Christ's crucifixion?

What I am about to present I do not give with dogmatic confidence. Rather, I suggest it as deserving of careful consideration. I am not laying down doctrine but am suggesting an interpretation of one way to see Elihu in Christ's sufferings. This is an analogy, not an allegory.

Consider with me the possibility that Elihu represents Satan's mental attack upon Christ in the final three hours of His passion.

Darkness fell upon the land during Christ's three final hours on the cross. All four of the Gospels are silent at that point, telling us nothing of what took place during those three dark hours. It's as though the Holy Spirit were saying, "I don't want to talk about it." The pain of the Godhead during those three final hours was immeasurable.

The Bible says nothing of this, but is it unreasonable to suppose that Satan would have tormented Jesus mentally during those lonely hours on the cross? Satan's attacks have always been against the mind. Surely Satan would have tried, up to the last moment, to dislodge Christ from His redemptive purpose while He hung on the cross.

Satan's Final Tactic

Those last three hours on the cross were Satan's last chance. If he could not successfully tempt Jesus to abort the process, Jesus would arise the Victor. Satan was watching Jesus pass every test successfully, and he was becoming frantic with the thought that Jesus would persevere all the way through to victory. So Satan poured his darkest, vilest attack upon Jesus in those final hours.

I believe the same thing was happening with Job. Job had endured the taunting accusations of his three friends, and he was persevering in the trial toward victory. So Satan launched his last and most insidious attack—Elihu.

By the end of Job 31, Satan is very nervous. Not only has he been unsuccessful in getting Job to curse God, he is watching God shape Job into a very dangerous vessel.

Satan launches one great final attack by mobilizing Elihu. He chooses a vessel that is young, passionate, articulate, and extremely bright, with enough self-confidence to speak boastful things.

Elihu represents Satan's last-ditch effort to unseat the saint from the path of righteousness. Elihu's speech is the last great torment that Job must endure before the glory of God's visitation. Elihu's weapon is his intellect. He is much brighter than Job's three friends, and much more capable at filling Job's mind with confusion and self-doubts.

The pain of his assault upon Job is exacerbated by the shrewdness of his mental capacities. In this regard Elihu is a counterpart to Satan, who is very adept at using his cunning to disorient the saints.

Satan always comes to God's people as an angel of light, pretending to be their advocate (2 Corinthians 11:14). Similarly, Elihu (whose name means "my God is He") pretends to be Job's friend and advocate. **"Truly I am as your spokesman before God; I also have been formed out of clay. Surely no fear of me will terrify you, nor will my hand be heavy on you"** (33:6-7). Elihu is making two claims: 1) he is the mediator for which Job had pined (see 9:33; 23:3-7). He has received revelation from God, and yet is also formed of human clay, so he qualifies as the spokesman or mediator between Job and God—a fairly strong boast; 2) he is claiming that he will handle Job gently with his tongue. But Elihu violates both claims. He is not a capable mediator, and he actually slashes Job more cruelly with his tongue than the others did.

Satan's customary tactic is to get to as close to the truth as he possibly can, and then use the truth as leverage to tempt the saint into sin. This is what he did at Jesus' temptation, for he quoted Scripture as the basis for his appeal to Jesus (Matthew 4:6). And this is Elihu's tactic with Job. Elihu uses his brainpower to articulate some very sensible arguments, but then he takes the truth of his statements and uses it as a sword to gouge Job.

Elihu's arguments are closest to the truth, which makes them the more painful. Satan knows how to use truth against us to full advantage. Elihu makes one of the greatest utterances of truth in 35:14, but then uses it in the next two verses to stab Job. This is Satan's way. *The greatest pain comes to the soul when truth is spoken to us but in such a way as to destroy and demean.* This tactic produces great mental suffering, for now Job must ask himself, "Is this really the way it is? This man seems to have such insight, there is such clear logic in his words, could he possibly be right? Am I in fact this wicked person he describes?"

We don't know the precise nature of Jesus' suffering on the cross, and it's admittedly conjecture to suppose that Satan launched a final mental attack against Jesus during His final three hours on the cross. But perhaps Jesus was hinting at something when He cried out toward the very end, "Eli, Eli, lama sabachthani?' that is, "My God, My God, why have You forsaken Me?" (Matthew 27:46). Are we going too far to suggest a possible connection between "Eli Eli" and "Elihu?" Surely Satan used all his intellect to assault Christ's mind on the cross—to try, with tormenting thoughts, to cause Christ to curse His Father.

Notice that Elihu is not called Job's friend, for Satan is not Jesus' friend. Elihu is called the friend of Job's three antagonists (32:3) for they had certainly partnered with his accusations, but he is not called Job's friend. In the end Job is restored in friendship to Eliphaz, Bildad, and Zophar—but not to Elihu. Elihu will never be Job's friend.

Up until noon, the soldiers, Pharisees, and people poured their venom upon Christ. When they settled into silence, Satan (Elihu) stepped up to the bat. The sun turned dark, and Jesus' blackest hours began as Satan poured out the equivalent of Elihu's six chapters of assault.

I've always wondered why Satan crucified Jesus when Jesus had clearly prophesied both His death and resurrection. On the surface, it appears as though Satan played right into Jesus' hand, stupidly fulfilling Jesus' prophecy by nailing Him to the cross. But Satan is no fool. Since the cross was Satan's downfall, why would he appear to cooperate with God's purposes so willingly? Perhaps the answer is in this, that Satan wanted a chance to attack Jesus' mind in the context of ultimate suffering. He had enough self-confidence in his ability to use truth as a sword, that even though he couldn't defeat Jesus in the wilderness, he thought he had a better chance of defeating Him in the place of great suffering. His design was to use Scripture and truth against Jesus while He was on the cross, to discourage His soul to the point of blaspheming God. But the prophet foretold that He wouldn't be discouraged unto blaspheming God: "He will not fail nor be discouraged, till He has established justice in the earth" (Isaiah 42:4).

Hallelujah! Jesus rose up the Victor! And so did Job.

9

Parallels To The Cross

My theology of years ago didn't see any connection between Job's sufferings and Christ's. But that has changed.
Now I see remarkable parallels between Job's and Christ's
sufferings. I'm not alone, for it was the practice in the
churches from the second century to read from Job during
Passion Week.[1]

Jesus said of the Old Testament Scriptures that "these
are they which testify of Me" (John 5:39). Consider with me
how the book of Job testifies to Christ and His sufferings:

1. The most righteous man on earth suffered the most of any man on earth.

This is true of both Job and Jesus. Job is the standard
for suffering in the Old Testament, and Jesus is the standard in the New Testament. Job's sufferings point prophetically to the Messiah, predicting that God's Blameless One
was going to suffer inexpressibly on our behalf.

2. Job did nothing wrong to deserve his suffering.

Nor did Jesus. Since neither man did anything evil to
deserve their suffering, our tendency is to look at their

---

[1] The Preacher's Homiletic Commentary: Volume 10, pages 5, 53, 80.

suffering and cry, "This is unjust!" In one sense that's true. If you view suffering as punishment for sin, then their suffering is totally unjust.

It is in this sense that it says of Christ, "He was taken from...judgment" (Isaiah 53:8). Jesus was deprived of justice when He was sentenced to the cross.

Now look at what it says about Job: **"Then the LORD said to Satan, 'Have you considered My servant Job, that there is none like him on the earth, a blameless and upright man, one who fears God and shuns evil? And still he holds fast to his integrity, although you incited Me against him, to destroy him without cause'"** (2:3). God testified here that Job suffered without an evil cause. It was unjust suffering.

Although some suffering appears to be unjust, however, God's justice will not be compromised. When a saint suffers unjustly, God's justice finds a way to turn that suffering into something redemptive, bringing good out of that which was intended for evil.

3. Job suffered so acutely so that men everywhere would be able to identify with him.

I've never met a saint who said, "Job's sufferings were nothing compared to what I've had to endure." No, virtually everyone feels that Job suffered as much or more than themselves. Herein lies the power of Job's apostolic example, because every sufferer is able to connect with Job, finding hope, encouragement, and faith in God's mercy to him. In this way Job's suffering was redemptive.

Similarly, no one can look at the cross and say, "Jesus doesn't know pain. He didn't hurt like I'm hurting. He can't relate to my pain." No one can talk like that. Literally anyone and everyone on the planet can look at Jesus' suffering and recognize that Jesus suffered as much or more than we have ever suffered. No one understands pain better than Jesus. He sank to the very dregs of human suffering so that now he might lift up the lowest of men to the heights of glory.

It's the fact that no one has suffered more than Job or Jesus that qualifies them to serve as examples for the entire human race. The greatest voice is not given to the untouched or unscathed, but to those who have experienced the pain of those to whom they're sent. *God will allow His servants to walk through pain so they will be anointed to speak to those who suffer thus.* Jeremiah did not deserve prison, but God allowed him to suffer the deprivation of prison so that he might be empowered to speak prophetically to the people about their impending imprisonment in Babylon. When the people ended up in captivity in Babylon, they were able to receive Jeremiah's ministry because he had lived where they were now living. The pain gave Jeremiah a platform for ministry impact.

Jesus could have exempted Himself from the painful consequences of our sin, but He chose to identify with suffering sinful humanity. Herein is the power of the gospel.

Though Job's suffering serves us today, even more so, Christ's sufferings avail for us today. Similarly, there are some today who are called to suffer for the sake of the body of Christ. Paul wrote, "I now rejoice in my sufferings for you, and fill up in my flesh what is lacking in the afflictions of Christ, *for the sake of His body,* which is the church" (Colossians 1:24). Paul found a purpose in his pain which went beyond the value of affliction to keep him humble or dependent or purified. He realized that his sufferings were for the purpose of benefiting the body of Christ. His weakness was ministering life to others, granting others the courage to persevere. Thus, the mighty apostle became relevant to the least and weakest of saints. Like Job, this is suffering with redemptive purpose.

4. It was God's will for Job to suffer.

God had profound purpose in Job's crucible, which we discuss at length in other portions of this book. Job's suffering was God's idea, not Satan's. This is proven by the fact that God mentioned Job's name to Satan, not vice versa. God picked the fight. Overarching Job's entire ordeal was God's sovereign will. God had a plan for producing great blessing out of Job's suffering.

Likewise, it was God's will for Jesus to suffer. One of the most amazing statements about Christ's sufferings is found in Isaiah 53:10, "Yet it *pleased* the LORD to bruise Him." God took pleasure in Christ's sufferings, not because of the pain, but because of the glory that would result.

Job participated in what the Scriptures call "sharing in the sufferings of Christ" (Colossians 1:24). What does it mean to share in Christ's sufferings? The answer to that is very important because not all sufferings are a sharing in Christ's sufferings. (There are such things as stupid suffering and senseless suffering.) Here's the answer I've come to as I've studied this question very passionately. *To share in Christ's sufferings is to "suffer according to the will of God"* (1 Peter 4:19). When God wills that we suffer in a certain manner for a certain season, He always has a redemptive purpose in it. Revelation 6:11 shows that there is a quantitative measurement of suffering that the church must fill before Christ will return. *The tears of Christ's bride water the soil of the endtime harvest.*

Sometimes you hear the voice, "You're just suffering your own private pain. Your suffering has no significance. Look at yourself, what is your painful little world accomplishing for anyone else? This is senseless suffering, it's pain without purpose. You are accomplishing nothing with your private little cross." This is what they would say to Jesus too, as He hung on Golgotha. "What do you think you're accomplishing with this?" But God has a way of taking our personal, private suffering, *and turning it into something that feeds the nations*—if we respond properly in it.

5. Suffering was God's pathway for Job to enter his higher inheritance.

Suffering was the only way Job could get his inheritance. He remained faithful in the trial and eventually received the promise (see Hebrews 6:15). Among many other high privileges, Job had the honor of establishing the first cornerstone of all sacred Scripture. He received a double portion of blessing and a place of great honor in God's redemptive purposes.

Suffering was also Jesus' pathway to promotion. The devil tempted Jesus by offering Him the honor of the nations without the agony of the cross (Matthew 4:8-9). But Jesus refused the easy way and, instead, set His face resolutely toward the cross.

As a result, Jesus has received a place of honor in heaven that is higher—if that were possible—than that which He knew before. "Therefore God also has highly exalted Him and given Him the name which is above every name, that at the name of Jesus every knee should bow, of those in heaven, and of those on earth, and of those under the earth, and that every tongue should confess that Jesus Christ is Lord, to the glory of God the Father" (Philippians 2:9-11). Incomprehensible glory now awaits the Lord Jesus Christ because He said yes to the pain.

This is a powerful principle: *God appoints His favorite ones to suffering.* Those who are called to the highest promotion are also appointed to the greatest suffering (see Acts 9:15-16).

Like Job, Christ became a spectacle in His suffering in order that through the reproach of His sufferings He might make a spectacle of the powers of darkness (Colossians 2:15).

6. Job asked why.

- **"Have I sinned? What have I done to You, O watcher of men? Why have You set me as Your target, so that I am a burden to myself? Why then do You not pardon my transgression, and take away my iniquity? For now I will lie down in the dust, and You will seek me diligently, but I will no longer be"** (7:20-21).
- **"I will say to God, 'Do not condemn me; show me why You contend with me"** (10:2).
- **"Why do You hide Your face, and regard me as Your enemy?"** (13:24).

In the crux of his pain, Job longed to know why. Jesus also asked why. We see this at the close of His ordeal on the cross: "And about the ninth hour Jesus cried out with a loud voice, saying, 'Eli, Eli, lama sabachthani?' that is, 'My God, My God, *why* have You forsaken Me?' (Matthew 27:46).

Do not rebuke the suffering saint who asks why. The Lord intends for us to grow in our understanding of why, but there are times when we just don't understand. The Scriptures invite us "to inquire in His temple" (Psalm 27:4). But it is important *how* you ask why. You must ask why in His temple. Don't go around questioning God to other people, that will quickly earn God's displeasure. If you have any questions, ask of Him directly to His face.

7. In his darkest hour, Job's friends failed him.

This seems to be a common denominator in the greatest of tests. It happened to Job, it happened to Jesus, and it still happens today. It's a vital part of the process of God forming the man, changing his wineskin, and preparing him for higher things.

In a limited way, Job's wife has a parallel to the disciples. Even as Job's wife was the closest person to his heart, so the disciples were the closest to Jesus.

Job was forsaken by the wife of his affections; Jesus was betrayed by a disciple with a kiss.

8. Job's sufferings had three sources: God's abandonment, Satan's assaults, and people's reproaches.

Jesus suffered from the same three-fold combination. Both Job and Jesus felt like they had all of heaven, hell, and earth ganged up against them. Let's look at these three elements in both lives.

God's abandonment:

- Job couldn't find God anywhere.
- Jesus cried out, "Why have You forsaken Me?"

Satan's assaults:

- Satan personally instigated Job's calamities and boils.
- Satan filled Judas, the Jewish leaders, and the Roman soldiers with an almost insane craving for Jesus' blood. Jesus said, "But this is your hour, and the power of darkness" (Luke 22:53)—the cross was clearly instigated by Satan.

People's reproaches:

- Job was reproached by his three friends. God vindicated Job in time, washing away his reproach and causing his acquaintances to acknowledge his honor.
- Jesus was reviled by the Jews, the Romans, and the robbers who were crucified with Him. But God has not yet vindicated Christ fully. There is a reproach

that Christ still carries before the unbelieving. As surely as God vindicated Job, God is going to vindicate Christ and wash away all His reproach. On the last day, this will be the Father's primary agenda—to vindicate His beloved Son before all of heaven, earth, and hell. In that day, the honor bestowed upon the beautiful Son of God will be unparalleled. It will have been worth the wait!

9. Job was falsely accused.

In his final tirade against Job, Eliphaz flung a litany of accusations: **"For you have taken pledges from your brother for no reason, and stripped the naked of their clothing. You have not given the weary water to drink, and you have withheld bread from the hungry. But the mighty man possessed the land, and the honorable man dwelt in it. You have sent widows away empty, and the strength of the fatherless was crushed. Therefore snares are all around you, and sudden fear troubles you"** (22:6-10). This is one of the most puzzling passages in the entire book. Not one of these accusations is true! In chapters 29-31, Job is going to answer each of these accusations, but as Job's friend surely Eliphaz would know he is accusing him falsely. He is creating accusations out of thin air, hoping that a stray arrow might land.

They did the same thing to Jesus, spewing accusations popcorn-style against Jesus, hoping that just one of their accusations would find legal grounds for crucifixion.

10. Job was challenged by others to save himself.

Job's three friends goaded Job to save himself. They basically said, "If you'll repent of your sin, God will forgive and heal you, and you can get past this thing and get on with your life. Repent, and *save yourself* any further grief!"

In this sense, Job's three friends represent the three categories of people who sneered at Jesus to save Himself:

1) The Jews:

"And those who passed by blasphemed Him, wagging their heads and saying, 'You who destroy the temple and build it in three days, save Yourself! If You are the Son of God, come down from the cross.' Likewise the chief priests also, mocking with the scribes and elders, said, 'He saved others; Himself He cannot save. If He is the King of Israel, let Him now come down from the cross, and we will believe Him'" (Matthew 27:39-42).

2) The Gentiles (Romans):

"The soldiers also mocked Him, coming and offering Him sour wine, and saying, 'If You are the King of the Jews, save Yourself'" (Luke 23:36-37).

3) The robbers:

"Then one of the criminals who were hanged blasphemed Him, saying, 'If You are the Christ, save Yourself and us'" (Luke 23:39).

One big difference between Job and Jesus in this instance is the fact that Jesus had the power to save Himself, Job didn't. No amount of repenting could save Job. All Job could do was wait on God and trust Him. And that was enough.

11. Job was resurrected from his sufferings to a ministry of intercession for his friends.

So was Jesus. When Jesus rose from the dead, He arose as an intercessor on our behalf: "Therefore He is also able to save to the uttermost those who come to God through Him, since He always lives to make intercession for them" (Hebrews 7:25).

In the same way, Job was raised up in the last chapter to be an intercessor even for those who had added affliction to his misery. Here's the reading:

> **And so it was, after the LORD had spoken these words to Job, that the LORD said to Eliphaz the Temanite, "My wrath is aroused against you and your two friends, for you have not spoken of Me what is right, as My servant Job has. Now therefore, take for yourselves seven bulls and seven rams, go to My servant Job, and offer up for yourselves a burnt offering; and My servant Job shall pray for you. For I will accept him, lest I deal with you according to your folly; because you have not spoken of Me what is right, as My servant Job has." So Eliphaz the Temanite and Bildad the Shuhite and Zophar the Naamathite went and did as the LORD commanded them; for the LORD had accepted Job. And the LORD restored Job's losses when he prayed for his friends. Indeed the LORD gave Job twice as much as he had before** (Job 42:7-10).

The crucible produced in Job a new authority in prayer and a new dimension of seeing his prayers answered.

The passage also suggests that whatever estrangement took place between Job and his friends during the season of affliction, through his prayers, Job's antagonists were restored to friendship status with him. This is what Christ has done for us as well! We who were His hateful enemies have now through His intercession become His friends.

Job didn't come out of the crucible simply with a new commitment to intercession, he came out with a new identity. Intercession wasn't something he did, it was something he was. In a similar way, Jesus came through His sufferings totally qualified to be an intercessor on our behalf.

I hope you've been edified to behold Jesus in the life of Job. But just because there are parallels between the two does not mean Job was perfect. Let's turn now and look at his failure.

10

Job's Failure

We have established that Job was blameless before God and man. But was he perfect? Did he respond perfectly to his calamity? The answer is no. Job was not perfect, nor did he handle his crisis without sin.

There is only one Man who has ever responded properly in the midst of the valley of the shadow of death, and He was called Jesus of Nazareth. No other human is capable of coming through the depths of the valley without sin.

Job got as high marks from God as any broken, weak, sinful man could hope to get, and yet he collapsed under the weight of his grief. *When we're in the crucible, God doesn't expect all of our responses to be perfect.* The purpose of the crucible, after all, is to bring imperfections to the surface. God is big enough to handle our fears, frustrations, yearnings, anxieties, depression, anger, and self-pity. Job wasn't perfect, and God had plenty of correction to bring to him. But God's final verdict on Job is that he was a loyal and righteous servant. God's pleasure is very evident in this man who had kept his face toward God through the greatest trial of his life.

If you look at Job and think, "I would never get angry at God like that," then you're deceived. You think too highly of yourself. You've never been angry at God because in His grace He has spared you that degree of calamity. But believe me, if He were to send it to you, you would get angry at Him. God expected Job to get angry at Him. It's part of the package. But He didn't expect him to stay angry. He expected him to seek earnestly, and find God in his calamity. When you find the face of God in your calamity, the anger is dealt with. You can't behold God's face and be angry with Him—He's just too beautiful!

Job Was Not Sinless

Job admits to having sin and iniquity: **"Why then do You not pardon my transgression, and take away my iniquity?"** (7:21). Job isn't claiming to be sinless; he's simply claiming that there is no one big ugly sin in his life that has incurred this judgment. He recognizes that all of us have iniquity—inner motives of the heart that fall short of God's glory. His question here is, "God, if You're judging me for my iniquity, why don't you forgive and heal me?"

- **"How many are my iniquities and sins? Make me know my transgression and my sin...For You write bitter things against me, and make me inherit the iniquities of my youth"** (13:23, 26).
- **"If I have covered my transgressions as Adam, by hiding my iniquity in my bosom"** (31:33).

So Job recognizes that he has iniquity within himself, he is not sinless. Iniquity refers to the evil bent of the human heart, that capacity within all of us to sin, the cavernous dark side of our hearts which we don't fully understand and from which ugly things will arise which we didn't even know were there. So while confessing that he has iniquity, Job insists: **"Far be it from me that I should say you are right; till I die I will not put away my integrity from me"** (27:5).

Job is not sinless, but he maintains his integrity. That can appear to be a contradiction, so we need to understand what Job means by integrity. For Job, integrity refers to an uprightness of heart which purposes to follow righteousness and turn from evil. Integrity maintains a pure conscience through prompt repentance and godly behavior—to the best of one's knowledge. Job has a clear conscience, so he will not lie and concoct some grievous sin.

Job's Mouth

There are two points where it says Job did not sin:

- **In all this Job did not sin nor charge God with wrong** (1:22).
- **But he said to her, "You speak as one of the foolish women speaks. Shall we indeed accept good from God, and shall we not accept adversity?" In all this Job did not sin with his lips** (2:10).

But after chapter 3, it never again says that Job responded without sin. When the crucible became seemingly endless, Job's soul collapsed, and in the despair of his humanity he opened his mouth and began to vent his agony of soul. The Holy Spirit testifies, "In the multitude of words sin is not lacking, but he who restrains his lips is wise" (Proverbs 10:19).

Job felt like he had nothing more to lose, so he decided to open his mouth and articulate his pain. In contrast, it was said of Jesus, "He was oppressed and He was afflicted, yet He opened not His mouth; He was led as a lamb to the slaughter, and as a sheep before its shearers is silent, so He opened not His mouth" (Isaiah 53:7). It was in his many words that Job (as well as the other four men who spoke in the book) fell short of God's glory (Romans 3:23), and it is this which precipitates God's rebuke— **"Who is this who darkens counsel by words without knowledge?"** (38:2). God was saying, "Job, you don't know what you're talking about."

When God quizzed Job in chapters 38-41, He asked him many questions like, "Were you there when I created the worlds?" Or, "Do you understand the intricate wonders of the created order?" To every question Job had to answer, "No." And yet consider this: to every question Jesus would be able to answer, "Yes." Job, who knew so very little, opened his mouth. Jesus, who knew all, kept His mouth closed. Hmm, seems like a lesson here somewhere.

At the end, when Job beheld God's glory, he said, **"I lay my hand over my mouth. Once I have spoken, but I will not answer; yes, twice, but I will proceed no further"** (40:4-5). It required sovereign revelation to empower Job to quiet his tongue.

God further rebuked Job:

- **Moreover the LORD answered Job, and said: "Shall the one who contends with the Almighty correct Him? He who rebukes God, let him answer it"** (40:1-2).
- **"Would you indeed annul My judgment? Would you condemn Me that you may be justified?"** (40:8).

So God's indictment of Job is that he has rebuked God without knowledge and has annulled God's judgment by claiming God has not treated him fairly.

Delayed Judgment

There is a very important principle that Job is going to learn in the crucible, but he has not yet learned it: *Sometimes God delays judgment in order to promote His servants.* It is Job's lack of understanding in this principle that causes him to accuse God of injustice. It's a common fault still today.

With God, there is a great chasm between "denied justice" and "delayed justice." Many accuse God of denying them justice, when in fact He was delaying justice in order to test their hearts. Many forfeit what could have been theirs. They could have had justice after the delay, but because they became bitter, their justice became denied.

Here is the justice in the Job crucible: God intends to promote Job to a much higher place of intimacy and influence in the kingdom. But if He gives Job the promotion without the pruning, Job will self-destruct through spiritual pride. It's the undeserved distress that turns up the flame, and it's the flame that will save Job from himself. The delaying of justice is the very thing that qualifies and prepares Job for the higher place. No delay, no promotion. To get immediate justice means to forfeit the promotion. The delay is painful, but God in His justice has determined that the value of the promotion surpasses the pain of the delay.

You don't become a symbol of Christ's cross and a blessing to all generations without a pricetag. If you want the higher inheritance, the pricetag comes with it.

Job was being proven in the principle of Psalm 18:25, "With a blameless man You will show Yourself blameless." Job was blameless, and yet he was given ample opportunity to doubt this truth. It seemed so easy to blame God, especially when Satan was accusing God to him. But because he persevered with love in the face of God, he was able to ultimately see how God was blameless in all His dealings with him. *God was blameless in this: He rewarded Job in the end with a higher place in Him that excelled all the pain of the crucible.*

It is this principle which Jesus is illustrating in the following parable:

Then He spoke a parable to them, that men always ought to pray and not lose heart, saying: "There was in a certain city a judge who did not fear God nor regard man. Now there was a widow in that city; and she came to him, saying, 'Get justice for me from my adversary.' And he would not for a while; but afterward he said within himself, 'Though I do not fear God nor regard man, yet because this widow troubles me I will avenge her, lest by her continual coming she weary me.'" Then the Lord said, "Hear what the unjust judge said. And shall God not avenge His own elect who cry out day and night to Him, though He bears long with them? I tell you that He will avenge them speedily. Nevertheless, when the Son of Man comes, will He really find faith on the earth?" (Luke 18:1-8).

Jesus is showing us that sometimes God delays giving His people justice. He has a good purpose for the delay which they usually don't understand. But in His mercy toward them, "He bears long with them"—knowing that the delay will bear dividends if they will persevere in love. When the fullness of time comes and the process is complete, Jesus fervently tells us what God will do: "I tell you that He will avenge them speedily." When God determines that it's time for the deliverance to be manifest, He will perform it "speedily!" You might have to wait for a long time, but everything will change in a moment of time!

Jesus' final question in the passage is haunting: "Nevertheless, when the Son of Man comes, will He really find faith on the earth?" Central to the preparation of endtime apostles and leaders will be this issue of delayed justice. True faith perseveres in the face of delayed justice. Jesus is asking, "When I season my endtime servants with delayed justice, will I return to find them standing firmly in faith, waiting expectantly upon Me even when it seems that justice has abandoned them?" I pray the answer is yes.

So to summarize Job's greatest sin: He accused God wrongly of denying him justice. He did not understand that God's delayed justice was God's means to the greatest promotion. But because Job stayed relentlessly in God's face, God brought him through to overcoming faith and inflamed love and enlarged understanding. Oh, this is awesome stuff!

11

Embracing God's Discipline With An Open Spirit

Here's the central premise of this chapter: *When you begin to see purpose in the crucible, you can embrace God's dealings with an open spirit.*

One of the greatest challenges of the Job crucible, however, is to see purpose—divine purpose. God has a purpose for your valley, and it's absolutely crucial that you uncover it.

God's Purpose In Job's Sufferings

In Chapter Three, while describing my "hermeneutical lens" for interpreting the book of Job, I made this statement about God's purposes: *"The purpose of the calamity is to glorify God by changing Job and bringing him to a higher spiritual inheritance."*

There is profound purpose in the book of Job. When you find yourself in the Job crucible, it is critical that you discover purpose. You must see the Job crucible as God's way of bringing you to higher dimensions of spiritual attainment than you ever thought possible.

The purpose of Job's sufferings is very strong and compelling, but if you don't see it, you are left to fatalism. For example, Janice E. Catron, in summarizing her understanding of Job, writes this:

"For many, the ending is ultimately unsatisfactory. The ending treats Job as if all his grief over his former children and servants magically disappears with his new circumstances. Certainly the ending does not answer the question of why bad things happen to innocent people. We are still left to wonder: Why did Job have to suffer so much? Why did the children and servants have to die? What about justice for them? How can a 'good' God allow (or cause) these things?"[1]

When you understand the book of Job, you want to cry out to these kind of commentators, "NO!! You don't get it!" There is no question in my mind why Job had to suffer so much. *God promoted him to the place of being a spiritual father to all saints of all generations who have walked through the valleys of God's refining fires. The excellence of that inheritance could be bought only at* a great personal price, even as the excellence of Christ's inheritance was bought at the greatest personal price. Even the taking of Job's first children was within God's mercy for it is possible that He saved them from a greater apostasy.

I am committed to declaring in this book that there is profound purpose in Job's sufferings, and exhilarating answers to those who share in the same fires.

Through God's grace, I believe it's possible to uncover purpose in *all* of life's tragedies. That's a bold claim because our world is overflowing with seemingly senseless suffering. Millions of people are dying prematurely for no apparent redemptive reason. But I believe that when we bring the brokenness of our lives to Christ, and submit the senseless suffering of our lives to His redemptive hand, that He has the power to imbue every tragedy with divine purpose.

Sometimes, when we come to Christ with our calamities, He miraculously turns our tragedies into triumph with

---

[1] Catron, Janice E., "Job: Faith Remains When Understanding Fails," HORIZONS Magazine, Volume 10, Number 3.

virtually no more effort on our part than a simple exercise of faith. In other instances, He intends that our pain launch us into an intense spiritual search until we are able to discover divine purpose in the calamity. That impassioned pursuit of God will produce more fruit in your life than if you received instant relief.

The international gospel of Jesus Christ declares that He has a purpose for your life, regardless of your broken-ness. This truth is found in Romans 8:28, "And we know that all things work together for good to those who love God, to those who are the called according to His purpose." God is able to work your greatest sufferings together for His good, as long as you fasten your love upon Him. You will see your circumstances in the light of "His purpose"—which, you may have noticed, is often very different from our purpose.

One of the greatest Bible illustrations of this truth is found in John 9, which is the account of Jesus healing the man who was blind from birth. The disciples asked Jesus, "Rabbi, who sinned, this man or his parents, that he was born blind?" (John 9:2). Jesus' disciples are reflecting the theology of Job's three friends, who were looking for a sin-ful cause to Job's sufferings.

When the disciples asked why this man seemed to be suffering so senselessly, Jesus brought purpose to the tragedy. He said to them, "Neither this man nor his par-ents sinned, but that the works of God should be revealed in him" (John 9:3). Still today it continues to be the work of God to bring purpose to the purposeless misfortunes of this pain-filled world.

When you begin to see God's purpose in your pain (a process which usually takes months and even years), then your spirit begins to open to the Father and the light of your countenance begins to glow. Excitement begins to build within you as you realize that He who began this good work in you is going to complete it!

What Is "An Open Spirit?"

The expression "an open spirit" is not found in the Bible, but the concept is substantiated scripturally. When we relate to someone else, we relate to that person with either an open spirit or a closed spirit. An open spirit embraces the other person freely even if the relationship is difficult; a closed spirit protects itself from the other person and relates to the other person with a measure of guarded distance or suspicion.

Jesus described a closed spirit within the marital relationship when He said, "Moses, because of the hardness of your hearts, permitted you to divorce your wives, but from the beginning it was not so" (Matthew 19:8). Hardness of heart within marriage is the same thing as a closed spirit. If your wife should ever close her spirit to you, sir, you're in trouble. That means she has hardened her heart because of the dynamics in the relationship, and now it will be very difficult to penetrate her defenses and truly be heard. Instead of hearing your heart, she'll hear everything you say through the jaded lens of her suspicions.

When one or both spouses has a closed spirit, nothing can be accomplished in helping the relationship until the hardness comes down, and the couple once again relates to one another with open spirits.

Here's another example of an open spirit: how kids relate to their parents in the disciplining process. When Paul taught on child discipline, he exhorted the fathers, "do not provoke your children to wrath, but bring them up in the training and admonition of the Lord" (Ephesians 6:4). A father might be right in bringing correction, but if he does it in a heavy-handed way, he can feel justified about the discipline he's meting out but end up provoking his child—and the child can end up closing his spirit to his father. It's vital, when disciplining our children, that we safeguard that "open spirit" relationship with them. If we sense them closing down to us, we must stop and gently pry them open.

Jonah's story illustrates that it's possible to obey on the outside and be closed down on the inside. Jonah eventually went to Nineveh, but he went with a closed spirit—which eventually manifested in his anger against God (Jonah 4). Some parents have been fooled by the outwardly submissive behavior of a compliant child, only to discover at a later time that the child's spirit had closed to them. Strong-willed children will close their spirits to you very quickly but will often open themselves back up just as quickly!

One of the greatest challenges of parenting is learning how to lead your children in the way of godliness while keeping their spirit open to you. Similarly, *God's heart in disciplining us is to correct us while gently challenging us to keep our spirit open to Him.*

A Closed Spirit

When God disciplines, we instinctively recoil and withdraw. If He corrects us real strongly, we'll even curl up emotionally into a fetal position. When we are filled with this kind of pain, our self-preserving instincts kick in because we feel like we're on data overload. "Much more of this, God, and you'll kill me!" And yet, in the midst of the crisis, the Lord assures us of His loving affection over and over.

When God disciplines hard, you will close your spirit. Even if you feel spiritually equal to the challenge, when the discipline actually comes, it can take your breath away in its unanticipated suddenness and severity. It's part of the process of God's most forceful seasons of discipline.

There are two ways people close their spirits when God disciplines hard. *Some close their spirit and actually turn away from God; others close their spirit while still continuing to serve God.* The former partner with the deceiver in accusing God, and they end up aborting and forfeiting the higher inheritance God intended for them. The latter still love God, but hold themselves back from the brightness of His countenance, and never totally unveil their faces in His presence for fear of what might come next. Job was at that place when he wrote, **"Therefore I am terrified at His presence; when I consider this, I am afraid of Him"** (23:15).

The book of Job chronicles the unfolding journey of a man who got disciplined hard by God, closed his spirit tightly to God, and then slowly began to open again to the Lord as he began to walk through the valley of the shadow of death. (The phrase "shadow of death" occurs nine times in the book of Job, so there's no question that David borrowed that phrase from Job's life when he used it in the most beloved Psalm. See Psalm 23:4.)

Initially, Job closes his spirit real hard, he curls up in a ball of pain, and curses the day of his birth (chapter 3). In the first several chapters, he is clearly holding God at arm's length. **"Have I sinned? What have I done to You, O watcher of men? Why have You set me as Your target, so that I am a burden to myself?"** (7:20). Instead of criticizing Job, we should see him as being transparently honest with his thoughts and feelings.

At first, Job can't see that God has a loving purpose in his calamities. He doesn't realize that he's suffering because of God's pleasure in him. But slowly, over time, God begins to unfold purpose to Job. So as the book progresses, we see Job's spirit beginning to open more and more to His God. *It's the revealing of purpose that enables Job to slowly open his spirit again to God.* Follow the progression with me through Job's nine speeches.

1. Job's first speech is one massive cry of unending pain (chapter 3).

When first disciplined, his spirit clamps shut and he cries out, **"Why is light given to him who is in misery, and life to the bitter of soul, who long for death, but it does not come?"** (3:20-21) Job's first speech is one massive cry of unending pain.

2. In his second speech, Job is trying to protect himself from God's probing gaze because he is terrified of God right now.

Job utters only grief and anguish. He relates to God very defensively and self-protectingly, which are evidences of a closed spirit. Here's how Job expresses it:

> **"What is man, that You should exalt him, that You should set Your heart on him, that You should visit him every morning, and test him every moment? How long? Will You not look away from me, and let me alone till I swallow my saliva? Have I sinned? What have I done to You, O watcher of men? Why have You set me as Your target, so that I am a burden to myself? Why then do You not pardon my transgression, and take away my iniquity? For now I will lie down in the dust, and You will seek me diligently, but I will no longer be"** (7:17-21).

God seems to be acting more like an enemy than a friend.

3. Job's tenor perceptibly changes in his third speech (chapters 9-10).

He starts by saying, **"God is wise in heart and mighty in strength. Who has hardened himself against Him and prospered?"** This is the first moment after his illness that Job extols the Lord, magnifying God for His wisdom and strength. And while Job has closed his spirit to God, he recognizes that he cannot harden his heart toward the Lord and prosper; therefore, he is committed to the process of again opening his spirit to God. So in 9:4-10 he glorifies God for His all-surpassing power and authority. Then he continues his complaint, realizing that at his best he is still full of disgrace before God and in need of His mercy (see 9:15, 21; 10:15).

**4. In his fourth speech, Job's spirit is obviously open-
   ing to God more and more as he begins to see purpose in his crucible (chapters 12-14).**

Job extols the sovereign wisdom of God at length. Then
he makes what is probably his most-quoted statement:
**"Though He slay me, yet will I trust Him. Even so, I will
defend my own ways before Him"** (13:15). Job's spirit is
opening to God to the point where he expresses his complete trust in God even if God kills him.

He follows immediately with the first indication that he
believes God is going to save him from his calamity: **"He
also shall be my salvation, for a hypocrite could not
come before Him"** (13:16). Furthermore he adds, **"All
the days of my hard service I will wait, till my change
comes"** (14:14). These are the first indications that Job is
beginning to see *purpose* in his crucible. He is beginning
to realize that God intends to deliver him in the end, and
this hope enables him to open his spirit more and more to
God's hand upon his life. The process is not complete in
his heart, however, for he still requests that God withdraw
His hand from him (13:21) and look away from him (14:6).
These emotional and mental vacillations are typical ways
humans respond in their weakness to the process.

**5. In this next speech, Job expresses his exasperation
   with his friends who refuse to cease their merciless
   attacks (chapters 16-17).**

He describes many dynamics of his grief, and expresses
his distress over his friends' darkened understanding.

**6. Job, in his sixth speech, is growing in his realiza-
   tion that God intends to not only save him from
   his affliction, but also change him through a revolutionizing revelation of Himself (chapter 19).**

Job articulates his pain by describing the many ways God has afflicted and devastated him, but then his speech takes a dramatic turn as he ends the chapter with the most profound prophetic declaration of the entire book: **"For I know that my Redeemer lives, and He shall stand at last on the earth; and after my skin is destroyed, this I know, that in my flesh I shall see God, whom I shall see for myself, and my eyes shall behold, and not another. How my heart yearns within me!"** (19:25-27). Job is working with a strong prophetic anointing right here. He is perceiving in his spirit that God is intending to give him a magnificent revelation of Himself, and he realizes this revelation of God is going to come to him in this present life— **"in my flesh I shall see God."** This growing clarity of God's *purpose* is giving Job great yearning of heart; it's increasing hope, and the ability to open his spirit more and more to God.

7. Job declares that God's judgment awaits the wicked (chapter 21).

Job refutes his friends' contention that evil calamity comes upon the wicked. He philosophizes on how the wicked often prosper until the day of their death, but then he declares that God's judgment awaits them after death.

Job says this regarding the wicked: **"Neither is the rod of God upon them"** (21:9). Job points to the way the wicked often seem to prosper, with none of God's disciplines correcting their course in life. This word is true. God does not bring discipline to the wicked. His discipline is an expression of His love, and it is reserved for His sons (Hebrews 12:5-11).

8. The process continues but is not complete in Job's eighth speech because his spirit is still somewhat closed to God (chapters 23-24).

Job mourns the loss of his awareness of God's presence. He can't find God. And it's here that he makes another of his greatest statements: **"But He knows the way that I take; when He has tested me, I shall come forth as gold"** (23:10). Again Job is seeing *purpose* in the crucible, recognizing that God is using this calamity to purify him like gold. He is describing the two-fold purpose: character change **("as gold")**, and manifestation of deliverance power **("I shall come forth")**.

Understanding this doesn't lessen the pain, but it does give it significance. Even so, Job is still afraid of God's hand in his life: **"Therefore I am terrified at His presence; when I consider this, I am afraid of Him. For God made my heart weak, and the Almighty terrifies me"** (23:15-16). Job's terror of God is a mixture of both healthy fear and imbalanced fear. He owns a healthy fear of God's awesomeness and power, but he is still fearful of God's hand and dealings in his life.

9. Job's final speech is altogether glorious, showing a heart that is opening more and more to God (chapters 26-31).

From this point on, Job's friends have nothing more to say. With his friends reduced to silence, Job launches a 6-chapter monologue which will conclude his utterances. In chapter 26 he extols the magnificence of God; in chapter 27 he depicts the final dereliction of the wicked. In chapter 28, he eloquently declares that wisdom cannot be found or uncovered at man's initiative; wisdom is granted through God's initiative, and Job is implicitly suggesting that his crucible is intended by God to teach him wisdom. After Joseph came through this same crucible, he came out with an accelerated wisdom that enabled him to *"teach his el-ders wisdom"* (Psalm 105:22). Job realizes that one of God's *purposes* in the prison is to teach His servant wisdom—a reality which sustained Joseph in the darkness of his own prison (for Joseph most certainly knew Job's story).

Job ends chapter 28 with one of the most stellar state-ments of the entire book, a truth that will end up being quoted repeatedly in other portions of Scripture: **"Behold, the fear of the Lord, that is wisdom, and to depart from evil is understanding"** (28:28). In chapter 29 Job pines over the blessing and respect he once enjoyed. In contrast, chapter 30 describes his current pitiful condition and hu-miliation. Job ends his monologue (chapter 31) with an absolutely glorious description of what genuine godliness looks like, maintaining his integrity to the end (insisting that his calamity was not punishment for sin in his life).

Here's my point: throughout his pilgrimage of suffering Job grows in increasing understanding of God's purposes in the crucible, and the more he understands purpose, the more easily he can embrace God's hand in his life. But he is never free to fully open his spirit to God until God Him-self visits him in chapters 38-41. *It's the revelation of God that ultimately opens Job's heart completely to God's sover-eign purposes in his life.*

Job came through his crisis successfully by constantly lifting his face to God. While his friends talked about God, he talked to God. *Even when his attitude was carnal and his words careless, Job did one thing right: he kept himself in God's face.* This was the key that enabled God to lead Job to greater and greater understanding of purpose.

Scripture likens us to a lily (Song of Solomon 2:2). One of the qualities of a lily is that it will open in the light and close up its petals in the darkness. When we first hit the darkness we naturally close up. But like a lily, when we subject ourselves to the light of His presence, we will in-stinctively begin to open our spirit to Him. Job refused to turn away from the light of God's countenance, and

eventually God brought him to a place of complete openness to Himself.

When we commit ourselves to loving God with a dogged
determination in the midst of our pain, He will work all the
elements of our painful circumstances together for good—
because we're loving Him (Romans 8:28, "And we know that
all things work together for good to those who love God, to
those who are the called according to His purpose"). Psalm
91:14 further testifies to this: "Because he has set his love
upon Me, therefore I will deliver him."

*Even though we may flinch and wince before God when
the pain of His rod is freshly upon us, if we will persevere
in His face, He will bring us forward into the openness of
unveiled love* (2 Corinthians 3:18). Our goal is the absolute
abandonment of our beloved Lord Jesus Christ, who at the
time when God was literally killing Him, did not withhold
any part of His spirit from His Father but instead prayed,
"Father, into Your hands I commit My spirit." Jesus died
with an entirely open spirit.

Paul uncovered something of this secret, for he wrote,
"Therefore I take pleasure in infirmities, in reproaches, in
needs, in persecutions, in distresses, for Christ's sake. For
when I am weak, then I am strong" (2 Corinthians 12:10).
*It's one thing to persevere in tribulation, it's quite another
thing to "take pleasure" in tribulation! This is called embracing God's discipline with an open spirit.* Paul didn't attain
that openness overnight, but as God unfolded purpose to
him, he was slowly able to open his spirit to God in the
midst of the crucible.

Perfected Love

The Bible uses another term to describe an open spirit:
"perfect love." Perfect love is the kind of love that is able
to embrace God's hand in our life, regardless of its severity, without withholding ourselves from Him or closing our
spirit in the least. Perfect love realizes that anything from

God's hand is for our best, and it comes to us in the everlasting love of our Father who is absolutely "head-over-heels nuts" about us! So if He gives it, I can embrace it with an open spirit. Once we attain that place, we have attained perfected love.

Love has been perfected among us in this: that we may have boldness in the day of judgment; because as He is, so are we in this world. There is no fear in love; but perfect love casts out fear, because fear involves torment. But he who fears has not been made perfect in love (1 John 4:17-18).

What John is saying is, he who fears the discipline of God in his life is not yet perfect in love. I've heard Christians say things like, "Don't ask God for patience—everything crashed in my life when I asked for patience." Or they might say, "I've learned not to ask God for more Christlikeness." These kinds of statements are viewing God's disciplines from a closed spirit. This is not perfect love.

Ask. Ask big. Ask for the highest. Pray dangerous prayers! Go for the gold.

I hear God saying to Job, "Job, I am going out of my way to do something very extraordinary in your life. If you will cooperate with Me, I will bring you out into a totally new and broad place in Me. But to get there, you're going to have the honor of identifying with My Son's sufferings in a most singular way. I am inviting you to share the cross with My Son. I am giving you the opportunity to discover what extravagant love is all about. I am opening my Spirit to you, now open yours to Me!"

As Job saw the Father's purpose in the crucible, his spirit slowly opened to God more and more, and his love was made increasingly perfect. This perfected love thus becomes the greatest pursuit of all saints— "that Christ may dwell in your hearts through faith; that you, being rooted and grounded in love, may be able to comprehend with all the saints what is the width and length and depth and height—to know the love of Christ which passes knowledge; that you may be filled with all the fullness of God" (Ephesians 3:17-19).

12

Holy Desperation

"Do you intend to rebuke my words, and the speeches of a desperate one, which are as wind? Yes, you overwhelm the fatherless, and you undermine your friend" (6:26-27).

Here Job calls himself, "a desperate one." Job had been reduced to a place of holy desperation—a condition I want to describe in this chapter.

Not long ago I read a magazine article written by an American missionary who had visited Mathare, Nairobi. Mathare is a city within the city of Nairobi, Kenya; it's a slum city. Approximately 180,000 people live in Mathare in abject poverty. Nairobi has 60,000 street children, and many of them are from Mathare.

When the missionary (Randy Hurst) wrote about his first encounter with the children of Mathare, he said the thing that struck him immediately was their "desperate gaze." These children, living in a subsistence reality, were desperate—for food. This white missionary represented to them a possible source of money or food.

Randy was so touched by the needs of these children that he longed to move out into Mathare and minister to them. His host, however, strictly warned him to stay within the confines of the compound. "Those people are desperate,"

he said, and as a result crime is rampant. It's the desperation of hunger.

A Cry For More

Perhaps you have prayed, "Lord, make me hungry for
You," or perhaps you've even asked God to make you desperate for Him. I believe those are good things to ask, but
we're rarely prepared for how God answers them.

All of us instinctively collect comforts around ourselves
to make our lives as free of stress and pain as possible.
That's normal and not necessarily wrong. However, some
of us have become so comfortable with the good things of
this life that we don't feel a compelling need for God's help
and intervention. Often, it takes a sovereign act of God to
pull out from under us the props that keep us comfortable. We pray, "Lord, make me desperate for You," but then
when He removes our support system, we say, "That's not
what I meant, Lord!"

God knows how to make us desperate for Him. He knows
how to place a cry deep within our souls. He puts the cry
there with the intention of answering it. Perhaps no one in
the Bible illustrates this truth better than Hannah.

Elkanah had two wives, Hannah and Peninnah. Peninnah had children, but God had closed Hannah's womb. And
because Elkanah loved Hannah most, Peninnah showed her
hatred for Hannah by antagonizing her for her barrenness.
Hannah couldn't understand why God had seemingly cursed
her with childlessness, and she wept often in utter grief.
Finally, Hannah became so desperate for a baby that she
uttered an absolutely crazy prayer. She said, "God, if you'll
give me a son, I'll give him back to You!" No mother in her
right mind would give up the child she so longs to raise, but
Hannah had been brought to such a place of desperation by
God that she was willing to give her son back to Him.

God said, "That's the prayer I've been waiting for!" When
Hannah became that desperate, God opened her womb,

and she gave birth to the mighty prophet Samuel. God needed a Samuel, and in order to get His Samuel He made a woman desperate through barrenness. Sometimes we don't understand why our fruitfulness seems to be cut off, but *God will bring spiritual barrenness in order to produce the kind of desperation that will make us totally available to His purposes.*

Blessed are the hungry; blessed are the desperate.

Your hunger determines how hard you seek God. "The person who labors, labors for himself, for his hungry mouth drives him on" (Proverbs 16:26). There are levels of hunger, and there are levels of desperation. Some people think they're desperate for God, but really they're very happy with most things in their lives. *When God makes you absolutely desperate for Him, He turns your life totally upsidedown.*

Job Was Made Desperate

Just as God made Hannah desperate, He also made Job desperate. **"Do you intend to rebuke my words, and the speeches of a desperate one, which are as wind?"** (6:26).

When God makes you desperate for Him, all the rules change. Your life is totally out of your control; you have radically different values; you don't care what others think of you; you become extremely focused on your goal; relationships take a secondary role to your one pursuit; you will take great risks because you have nothing to lose; if anyone tries to stop you, you'll run over them. You're desperate.

Job's friends don't know what to do with this desperate man. He's different, and they don't understand the changes. He is nothing like the Job they once knew. They're saying to each other, "We can't talk to the guy; we can't reason with him; he won't receive anything from us. What's wrong with him? Does he think we're all wrong and he's right?" So they have no idea what to do with this man who was once their friend but who now seems to be living on another planet. They don't fully understand that their friend is now a desperate man.

Take it from me: *When you get thrown into a desperate pursuit of God, all your relationships change.*

Grace For The Race

A brother in Christ once said to me, "I want to pursue Jesus with that kind of desperation, but I just don't do it. I can't seem to do it on my own initiative. I always take the lazy way out, and then I get down on myself for being so passive in my pursuit of Christ. What can I do about that?"

It's my personal opinion that virtually all of us gravitate toward a more relaxed pursuit of God when everything is going well in our lives. To access this kind of desperation requires an act of grace. We don't have the inherent resources to touch it on our own. We need help.

I have defined grace as "God reaching out to man." Grace is God taking the necessary initiative to draw man unto Himself. It is grace and grace alone that causes man to raise a desperate cry to God, and then it is grace that empowers man to respond and take hold of God. *In other words, our coming into the higher things of God is totally His initiative.* All we can do is express our need and cry to Him for help. How He answers that cry is all of grace.

What Was Job Desperate For?

I've asked the question, "What was Job desperate for?" Well, for starters, he was desperate to be healed. When Job described his illness, it wasn't simply something that made him feel uncomfortable; it was literally life-threatening.

If you've ever known life-threatening infirmity, you understand the desperation that says, "I've *got* to get well!" This is why many people will travel incredible distances to visit a doctor they think can help them.

Job pursued God hard because he was desperate to be healed. But he was desperate for more than that. A mere healing would not satisfy Job. Job was too deep into this thing to be placated with just a physical healing. He had lost his ten children! A physical healing would not answer that loss.

Job was desperate for something far higher; he was desperate for a revelation of God! God had come to him as "the God who fries your theological circuits," and now everything Job had ever thought about God was in question. Job was saying, "Who are You anyways?? I don't think I even know You. Show me Your glory; I've got to see You for who You really are!"

As Job persevered in the crucible, he began to perceive something through prophetic discernment. *He came to realize that God had afflicted him with the specific intention of revealing Himself to him.* Job announces this confident assertion in what is perhaps the most dramatic prophetic declaration of the entire book: **"And after my skin is destroyed, this I know, that in my flesh I shall see God, whom I shall see for myself, and my eyes shall behold, and not another. How my heart yearns within me!"** (19:26-27).

Job is saying, "God didn't bring me into the valley to leave me there. He brought me into the valley in order to lead me up onto the mountain. God has shown me that there is a day coming when I shall see God on the mount—and that day will come before I die, while I am still in my flesh." Imagine the thrill and anticipation with which he added, **"How my heart yearns within me!"** He knew He was headed for a mighty revelation of God, and he could hardly wait for it to come!

It turns out that Job was right. God did in fact come in chapter 38 and reveal Himself to Job. If you find yourself in the Job crucible, then hear this: He's going to visit you, too!

The four chapters in which God spoke to Job (chapters 38-41) are more than simply a series of questions dictated

to Job in a sterile sort of manner. There was more happening to Job than simply the transfer of data. Job was in the
immediate presence of God Himself, and this encounter
with God shook him to the very depths of his being. Job
had longed for this moment, but when it finally came he
was totally blown away with the majesty and splendor and
beauty and power that overwhelmed his senses.

*With every question He asked of Job, God was not only
stilling Job's questions, He was revealing Himself in all His
omnipotent sovereignty.* Job's soul had ached desperately
for this moment, and it had finally come!

13

Seeking Fervently

God's purpose in making you desperate for Him is that you might seek Him more fervently than you ever have in all your life. *It's the impassioned pursuit of God that changes us.* "And you will seek Me and find Me, when you search for Me with all your heart" (Jeremiah 29:13).

Here's what this kind of desperate seeking looks like:

- You turn away from the fulfillment of social relationships with other people and are driven into the secret place of solitude with God where you seek His face. **"And he took for himself a potsherd with which to scrape himself while he sat in the midst of the ashes"** (2:8). *(Nobody resorts to the ashes of solitude with God on their own volition, they are driven there in desperation.)*
- You devour the Bible as food for a dying man. You search the Scriptures from cover to cover, frantically scouring the pages and tunneling into every verse for life-giving manna. (The Scriptures become manna for us when the Holy Spirit quickens the sacred writings to our heart by His awesome power.) These small fragments of God-breathed manna become your survival and source of sanity.

- You spend wholesale chunks of time staring at God, waiting upon Him in prayer and vigilant contemplation. "Behold, as the eyes of servants look to the hand of their masters, as the eyes of a maid to the hand of her mistress, so our eyes look to the LORD our God, until He has mercy on us" (Psalm 123:2). You believe that exposing yourself to His fiery presence will bring the change for which you pant. Job's friends **"sat down with him on the ground seven days and seven nights, and no one spoke a word to him"** (2:13). They joined Job in seven days of silent staring, but for Job this was a long-term commitment.
- Spiritual disciplines such as fasting, solitude, and self-denial are used gratefully as the gifts God intended them to be—vehicles which enable us to intensify our pursuit of Christ. Referring to fasting, Job said, **"I have not departed from the commandment of His lips; I have treasured the words of His mouth more than my necessary food"** (23:12).

Few have been driven to this desperation, and thus few have known the life-transforming power of this kind of seeking after God.

The Great Theological Tension

Job articulates a great theological tension which is of critical importance in maintaining a passionate pursuit of God. *Theology dictates behavior.* What you believe in this theological tension will determine whether you seek God passionately to the desired fulfillment, or whether you give up prematurely and abort God's purposes in the crucible.

Here's the tension articulated:

"For I know that my Redeemer lives, and He shall stand at last on the earth; and after my skin is

destroyed, this I know, that in my flesh I shall see God, whom I shall see for myself, and my eyes shall behold, and not another. How my heart yearns within me!" (19:25-27).

On the one hand, Job knew that his Redeemer would stand at last on the earth. This is a reference to the last day when human history is consummated and Christ stands on the earth as the victorious King, Bridegroom, and Judge. In that day, every wrong will be made right; every broken thing will be mended; every tear will be dried; every imperfection will be turned into perfection. Each one of us longs for that Great Day when all the shattered dreams of this imperfect order will be replaced with the glorious restoration of all things and the manifestation of the sons of God. Oh, come Lord Jesus!

On the other hand, Job was announcing that he was going to have a life-changing encounter with God in his flesh, in this life.

Most of us have wrestled with this question, "Should I contend for God's salvation to come to this particular situation in the here and now, or should I wait patiently for the time when all will be made whole at the return of Christ?" Your theology on this point is vitally crucial. Let me explain that by pointing to two theological extremes which are equally deadly:

The Deadly Nature Of Microwave Theology

"Microwave theology" says that it's God's will to heal, deliver, provide, and restore—*now*. When someone with microwave theology prays for you, they are expecting you to be healed immediately. And if you're not healed on the spot, they get mad at you.

In their minds they're thinking, "I just prayed the prayer of faith for you. Why haven't you received? I know I did my part; I prayed a faith-filled prayer. So if you haven't received, it's because you're living in unbelief or some other kind of sin."

If you have microwave theology, and you're not healed or delivered within your time frame, your soul will collapse. You'll begin to think, "I guess I don't have enough faith." Or you might think, "I am simply incapable of touching God in this thing, I just don't have what it takes." Or even worse, you might begin to partner with the accuser and think to yourself, "God hasn't fulfilled His Word! In my case, He has not held true to His promises. This business of believing God and standing on His Word doesn't work."

When the person with microwave theology doesn't get an immediate provision from God, he will conclude that he can't touch Jesus in the thing, and he'll give up. He'll collapse into numb resignation and decide he's just going to have to live with his problems.

In other words, he abandons the passionate pursuit of God. Since it didn't happen according to his timetable, he steps out of the race and becomes a coping Christian.

And that's exactly what Satan was lobbying for! It's Satan's design that the saint who is in the Job crucible abandon the hope of touching God and resign himself to apathetic, status quo Christianity. Microwave theology is deadly because it causes us to give up.

The Deadly Nature of Martha Theology

"Martha theology" is equally deadly because it has the same net effect of causing us to give up, but the reasoning is different.

Jesus said to Martha, "Your brother Lazarus will rise again."

Martha replied, "I know that he will rise again in the resurrection at the last day" (John 11:24).

Jesus responded in so many words, "No, Martha, you don't get it. You don't have to wait until the resurrection at the last day, because you have standing before you the

One who is Himself the resurrection and the life!"

And then, to validate His point, Jesus proceeded to raise Lazarus from the dead.

Before raising Lazarus, Jesus had to correct Martha's theology. She had an after-life theology, a theology that said everything will be fixed and healed and restored at the last day. Jesus rebuked Martha's theology by demonstrating His purpose to bring resurrection power to the ills of this fallen world in the here and now.

People with Martha theology will find ways to substantiate with Scripture that it's not God's will to deliver them. They believe that God will receive the highest glory through their life if they're not delivered in the here and now. While it's true that God is glorified through our patient endurance in the midst of suffering, it's tempting to adopt Martha theology so that we don't have to wrestle with our unbelief.

If you have Martha theology, you will decide that your present crisis is probably not going to get fixed in this life, you will gather yourself emotionally and brace yourself to live with your pain until Jesus returns. You will decide it's not God's will to heal or restore your particular problem, and you will give up the zealous pursuit of touching Jesus' garment in the thing. The despair of this kind of fatalism will reduce you to the passivity of status quo Christianity.

And again, that's exactly what Satan is campaigning for! He wants you to give up that desperate, passionate, hot pursuit of Christ until you lay hold of Him. He doesn't care if it's microwave theology or Martha theology that punctures your spirit, he just wants you to succumb to numb resignation and give up the driving edge of your pursuit.

Jacob Theology

There is another option, however! I call this "Jacob theology," because it was Jacob who said, "I will not let You go unless You bless me!" (Genesis 32:26). This is a theology that says, "I'm going to come after Jesus, I'm going to chase after Him with everything that is within me, and I'm not going to give up—ever. I'm going to hold on to the promise; I'm going to stay in His face; I'm going to seek His resurrection power *because I know it's available to me.* I know that the power of the cross can be accessed. I know that the resurrection power of Christ is intended by God to be manifest here on earth. I don't understand why I haven't been able to touch Him in this thing yet, but I'm not giving up until I do. And if I die while trying, that's God's business. But as long as there's breath in my carcass, I'm coming after Jesus with every ounce of strength I've got. I must gain Christ!"

That's the unrelenting determination of the saint who is embracing the Job crucible properly. This kind of tenacity makes for what is called a dangerous Christian. *This is the kind of saint that causes the minions of hell to shake in fear and trepidation, for they are beholding another Job—a man or woman who is determined to persevere in the face of God until He completes His purposes in their life.* Once this saint emerges from the crucible, he will come out with the kind of brokenness and consecration to God's purposes that will be unaffected by the schemes of the devil. He will truly be a vessel prepared by God for His endtime purposes in the earth.

Job's crucible testifies that you can have it all. You can be both changed and healed! You can be changed in the fire and delivered through His glorious power. You can buy eternal treasure in the fire and gain a testimony in the end of God's resurrection power. *If you turn the pain of your crucible into a passionate, desperate, relentless pursuit of Christ, you can have it all!*

14

Commitment To Integrity

The Job crucible is intended to launch us headlong into a passionate pursuit of Christ, but there is one other factor in addition to the desperate pursuit that is absolutely necessary if we are to gain the heights of spiritual promotion: we must safeguard our moral purity. In this chapter we will explore Job's profound commitment to personal purity.

Job's friends each offer three speeches throughout the book. As the three sequences of speeches unfold, Job's friends gradually run out of arguments. By the end of chapter 25, they had nothing more to say because Job was righteous in his own eyes.

As Job's friends are rendered silent, Job launches a six-chapter soliloquy (chapters 26-31). These chapters build toward the climax of Job's argument, much like the finale of a Tchaikosvki symphony. This is Job's great and final cry. By the time Job gets to chapter 31, he is concluding his complaints and declarations with incredible intensity— the trumpets are on their feet, the violin bows are whirling, the trombones are bellowing, the saxophones are blowing gaskets, the crash cymbals are assaulting the air, and the timpani are shaking the walls with their pounding thunder. Chapter 31 is the most awesome, definitive, conclusive, emphatic, mouthstopping passage in the entire book. It's an absolutely fantastic conclusion to a gripping confrontation of epic proportions. Let the music play!

Three Motifs Of Chapter 31

Through Holy Spirit inspiration, Job is going to simultaneously do three things for us in chapter 31:

1. He is going to validate his integrity beyond all doubt by listing his personal standards of holiness and good works.

Throughout the book, Job contends that if he has conducted himself in a wicked manner, he is certainly deserving of God's judgment. But he's going to conclude by underscoring that point, claiming in no uncertain terms that he is "not guilty" of great transgression and, thus, not deserving of the judgment he's known. In his conclusion he basically says, "Okay, guys, let me tell you how I've lived. You've accused me of wrongdoing, but now I will itemize for you my committed lifestyle of purity, love, and good works."

2. He is going to delineate the high water mark of true piety, defining godliness for all generations.

The prophet Micah asked this soul-searching question, "What does the Lord require of us?" Job 31 is the answer. As the first Bible book written, Job launches Scripture with a definitive statement on the nature and priorities of true godliness. Ever afterward, men of all generations would look back to Job 31 as the litmus test of genuine religion, the standard of godliness against which to measure our practices and priorities.

3. He articulates the major themes that will carry the endtime bride's heart as she prepares for her Bridegroom.

As the prophet of genuine piety, Job is showing us that the ancient spirituality will become the endtime spirituality.

After we have explored all the crevasses of what men can do to please God, we will return to the ancient standard of Job 31. The endtime bride will be established in a tenacious commitment to character and good works. *Job's pounding finale details the passionate heartbeat of the bride in the last hour as she has adorned herself with good works as with a wedding garment, in order to hasten and welcome the return of her Beloved and Friend.*

The moral convictions of Job 31 will not be peripheral niceties, but these values will be so burned into the fabric of her being that they will comprise the very DNA of that which the bride genetically reproduces in the newborn babes. These standards of godliness will be more than just what she does, it will be who she is. *And it will be her passion for holiness that will empower the bride to persevere through the hour of testing (the Job crucible) that is coming upon the whole earth (Revelation 3:10).*

Exhortations To The Endtime Bride

There are several ways we could approach chapter 31, but here's how I want to do it. I will take each aspect of Job's commitment to righteousness and articulate it as a personal exhortation to you, the reader. As you review this chapter with me, may the Holy Spirit tenderize your heart afresh to these truths. And may you allow Him to strengthen and reinforce the moral boundaries you have established as bulwarks of behavior around your life.

1. Guard the window to your thought life (31:1-4).

"I have made a covenant with my eyes; why then should I look upon a young woman? For what is the allotment of God from above, and the inheritance of the Almighty from on high? Is it not destruction for the wicked, and disaster for the

workers of iniquity? Does He not see my ways, and count all my steps?" (31:1-4).

Job starts by diving boldly into the issue of lust. There is a spirit of lust in the earth today that has been belched upon mankind from the cesspools of hell. It proliferates in the media, it continually assaults our senses, and it is central to hell's "holy war strategy" to snare and immobilize believers in the last hour.

Last days believers must encircle themselves with a perimeter of conviction in dealing with lust. *Mental purity must be more than a spiritual goal; it must be a personal passion that believers cherish as the priceless treasure of their hidden life.* Even when you have not attained perfection in an area (such as mental purity), you can still hold and guard it as a deep personal conviction.

The eye is the window to the thought life. Jesus said that with our eye we can fill our body with light or with darkness (Matthew 6:22-23). There is a war for the minds of young people today, and if we are to answer the attack, we must address the issue of pornography head-on.

The enemy doesn't mind if pornography stays underground. It gains its power in secrecy. Satan's scheme is to facilitate its secrecy, making it more readily available to our private lives. This scheme was greatly advanced with the advent of personal VCRs, videos, and cable TV.

Some Christian couples have justified using pornography in their bedroom. It is a great deception to think it can serve you to stimulate your marriage. You are compromising the perimeter around your home and family.

Just when we thought pornography couldn't become more secretive or proliferating, recent technology has caused it to literally explode around the world. I'm referring to the internet.

The packaging is new but the plot is ancient: snare the bride with the lust of the eyes. It is essential that we take aggressive, violent steps to establish boundaries of purity in our lives that will enable us to possess our convictions. I'm talking about violent things like quick repentance, transparent confession, disconnecting cable TV, refusing to watch R-rated videos period, canceling internet access— whatever it takes to establish moral purity in your thought life.

It is a matter of the bride being ready and adorned for the return of her Bridegroom.

2. Walk the narrow path of righteousness (31:5-8).

"If I have walked with falsehood, or if my foot has hastened to deceit, let me be weighed on honest scales, that God may know my integrity. If my step has turned from the way, or my heart walked after my eyes, or if any spot adheres to my hands, then let me sow, and another eat; yes, let my harvest be rooted out" (31:5-8).

Job is articulating a passion for truthfulness. He uses the words, **"walked," "foot,"** and **"my step."** He's talking about his life direction, about the practices of his daily walk. He has kept to the narrow path of uprightness and truth, careful lest his steps stray to the left or right.

Truth and honesty are intensely important to the end-time church. Consider these graphic verses at the very end of the Book:

- But the cowardly, unbelieving, abominable, murderers, sexually immoral, sorcerers, idolaters, and *all liars* shall have their part in the lake which burns with fire and brimstone, which is the second death (Revelation 21:8).
- But there shall by no means enter it anything that defiles, or causes an abomination or a lie, but only those who are written in the Lamb's Book of Life (Revelation 21:27).

- But outside are dogs and sorcerers and sexually immoral and murderers and idolaters, and *whoever loves and practices a lie* (Revelation 22:15).

3. Flee fornication (31:9-12).

"If my heart has been enticed by a woman, or if I have lurked at my neighbor's door, then let my wife grind for another, and let others bow down over her. For that would be wickedness; yes, it would be iniquity deserving of judgment. For that would be a fire that consumes to destruction, and would root out all my increase" (31:9-12).

In the first four verses Job talked about lust; now he talks about bodily sin. He calls bodily sexual sin **"a fire that consumes to destruction,"** a truth that Solomon picked up and expounded in the book of Proverbs.

Fornication is engaging in sexual activity with someone other than your spouse. Scripture is very clear that the only sexual activity God countenances is with one's spouse. All other sexual activity **"consumes to destruction."**

The church must be an uncompromising voice against the moral relativity of this generation. Some engaged couples justify premarital sex by saying, "We're getting married anyways." The truth is, you're not in covenant until you perform your vows and are united as one by God. People live together today without even blinking. God will judge His house so that there will be a marked difference in the last hour between the church and the world.

Dear believer, if you are having sex with someone who is not your spouse, you are decimating your uprightness before God. You're shooting your integrity to hell. You are playing the fool. You are sacrificing your integrity on the altar of personal satisfaction.

If you're living with someone who is not your spouse, repent and move out. If your boyfriend or girlfriend is putting pressure on you, break up. "But he says he loves me." No, he doesn't love you; he loves himself. If he loved you, he'd strive to help you safeguard your purity.

Perhaps you think I sound angry. I'm not angry; I'm terrified. "Knowing, therefore, the terror of the Lord, we persuade men" (2 Corinthians 5:11). We live in the presence of a God who has power to cast into hell. We will be perfected and purified only in the full-throttled fear of the Lord.

4. Treat others without discrimination (31:13-15).

"If I have despised the cause of my male or female servant when they complained against me, what then shall I do when God rises up? When He punishes, how shall I answer Him? Did not He who made me in the womb make them? Did not the same One fashion us in the womb?" (31:13-15).

In the immediate context, Job is speaking about how he handles his employees (servants). He is articulating his value for human life and the reality that all people are created as equals before God.

The endtime bride carries a passion against all forms of discrimination, whether based upon race or skin color or sex or social status or standard of living or language—or any such thing. Some are born into privilege; others are born into poverty, but we all stand naked before our great God and Creator.

Let us search our hearts. How do you relate to other employees who are less experienced than you, or less educated? Do you treat the disadvantaged as an equal? *Only when we view "the least of these" as being our equal will we be empowered by the Spirit to be a force for healing among the poor and hurting of the world.*

5. Help the poor, the widow, the fatherless (31:16-23).

"If I have kept the poor from their desire, or caused the eyes of the widow to fail, or eaten my morsel by myself, so that the fatherless could not eat of it (but from my youth I reared him as a father, and from my mother's womb I guided the widow); if I have seen anyone perish for lack of clothing, or any poor man without covering; if his heart has not blessed me, and if he was not warmed with the fleece of my sheep; if I have raised my hand against the fatherless, when I saw I had help in the gate; then let my arm fall from my shoulder, let my arm be torn from the socket. For destruction from God is a terror to me, and because of His magnificence I cannot endure" (31:16-23).

Most Christians are well taught in the principles of tithes and offerings (Malachi 3:8-12), but not all Christians have yet discovered the power of almsgiving. Alms are gifts given in secret to the poor (Matthew 6:1-4). Alms do not replace tithes but are given after the tithe has been given.

God is in the business of making us to be as broken bread given out for others—both naturally and spiritually. There is a certain release of kingdom power when we give secretly to the poor because of our passionate love for Jesus Christ. *Almsgiving was a passion for Job, and it will be restored to the endtime church as a passionately powerful way to express our love for Christ.*

There is a tendency for many to institutionalize this practice of helping the poor, the widow, the orphan, and the disadvantaged. What I mean is, we will put something in the offering plate at church and then expect the church as an institution to fulfill our responsibility. Or we'll give to a charitable organization like the Salvation Army and figure that we've dispensed our duty. But what Job practiced, and what Jesus taught, was the one-to-one giving of personal resources to a specific person or family in need.

Something profound happens when we practice biblical almsgiving. The abundance of thanksgiving causes the heart of the recipient to be joined to that of the giver, and the body of Christ is edified and joined together in the bond of love (2 Corinthians 9:12-14).

The Gentile church was birthed through the power of almsgiving. It was part of Cornelius's spiritual genetics which God chose to multiply in the nations (Acts 10:4). Job was passionately committed to this, as was Cornelius—and so, too, will be the endtime bride of Christ as she is poured out for the cause of Christ. *Our heart-felt compassion for the poor, widow, and fatherless will be a catalyst for opening the floodgates of heavenly visitation in the last hour.*

6. Guard against the love of money (31:24-25).

"If I have made gold my hope, or said to fine gold, 'You are my confidence'; if I have rejoiced because my wealth was great, and because my hand had gained much" (31:24-25).

It's interesting that this matter of money comes immediately after that of helping the orphan and the widow. One of the unique virtues of almsgiving revealed by Jesus is in its ability to purify the soul— "But rather give alms of such things as you have; then indeed all things are clean to you" (Luke 11:41). I asked the Lord what it was from which almsgiving made us clean, and I received the answer, "Greed." *Giving alms cleanses from the love of money.*

There is something about money that constantly seeks to encircle and wrap around our heart. No sooner have we gained new freedom from the love of money, then it grows around our hearts once again! Therefore, we must be constantly cutting back the undergrowth of greed's tentacles which seeks to recapture our affections. How do we do that? We do this through tithes in part, but even more significantly, through a lifestyle of offerings and almsgiving.

Even though Job was blessed with material substance, he kept a vigilant guard on his soul lest money should find a place in his heart. The endtime church must be fervently committed to this same principle of giving, for with each gift another encroaching tentacle of materialism is slashed back and thrown away.

7. Cultivate an exclusive passion for God (31:26-28).

"If I have observed the sun when it shines, or the moon moving in brightness, so that my heart has been secretly enticed, and my mouth has kissed my hand; this also would be an iniquity deserving of judgment, for I would have denied God who is above" (31:26-28).

By renouncing idolatry, Job is expressing his purposeful determination to love God first and foremost and exclusively.

This jealousy for an exclusive passion for Jesus is even now gripping the endtime bride. She is fervently committed to denying and crucifying all competing affections so that the Lord Jesus alone might shine in her heart as the light of her eyes.

Why do you think John closed his first epistle with the words, "Little children, keep yourselves from idols" (1 John 5:21)? Could it be because we all struggle with the constant temptation to place our affections upon things other than Christ?

Jesus told us what the greatest commandment was, "You shall love the LORD your God with all your heart, with all your soul, and with all your mind" (Matthew 22:38). I'm grateful to God that through Christ the great commandment becomes the great promise: He promises us that we "shall" love God with all our hearts! This is Christ's prophetic declaration over the church age that before He returns, the Holy Spirit will so empower us with holy affections for Jesus that we truly will love Him with wholehearted purity and exclusivity.

8. Forsake bitterness, bless your enemies (31:29-30).

"If I have rejoiced at the destruction of him who hated me, or lifted myself up when evil found him (indeed I have not allowed my mouth to sin by asking for a curse on his soul)" (31:29-30).

Nothing tests the spiritual mettle of a man more than how he responds to those who persecute him, hate him, despise him, reproach him, exclude him, or otherwise reject him. Jesus prayed for His enemies, and He instructed us to do likewise.

The endtime bride will have ample opportunity to have this dynamic tested in her heart. Many will hate her in the last days. She will face many chances to become angry. But she will carry Job's determination to guard his heart against all bitterness.

9. Be hospitable to strangers (31:31-32).

"If the men of my tent have not said, 'Who is there that has not been satisfied with his meat?' (but no sojourner had to lodge in the street, for I have opened my doors to the traveler)" (31:31-32).

Job's commitment to hospitality is a prophetic pattern that still speaks today.

The Scriptures admonish us to be hospitable to strangers (Hebrews 13:2; Matthew 25:35; Romans 12:13). This injunction is intimidating to some who have been taught to never trust strangers. To obey this Scripture, our trust in God must be stronger than our fear of exploitative people.

We must use godly wisdom and spiritual discernment and be willing to obey the Spirit's leading.

The spirit of Scripture militates against the individualism of our modern age. Many of us don't know our neighbors because our garage door opens automatically, we drive inside, the closer shuts the garage door upon us, and our privacy is preserved. Never mind attend to the needs of strangers, we don't even know our neighbors! The love of Christ, however, causes us to open to the needs and cares of others, even if it means our personal inconvenience.

10. Refuse to hide secret sin (31:33-34).

"If I have covered my transgressions as Adam, by hiding my iniquity in my bosom, because I feared the great multitude, and dreaded the contempt of families, so that I kept silence and did not go out of the door" (31:33-34).

Job is referring to the way Adam tried to cover his nakedness after he first sinned (Genesis 3:7). Ever since, men have acted just like their first ancestor. Fear causes us to hide and internalize our failures and sins. We are afraid of what others might think if they really knew who we were. And we also tend to think that we can cover up our sins from God Himself. How foolish!

Job is articulating a personal commitment to confess his sins openly and quickly. *The endtime bride will be ardently given to "radical repentance."* She will not allow sin to find any foothold in her heart but, instead, will deal violently with it by confessing it boldly to others and allowing the light of God's grace to dispel every shadow of darkness.

True Christian character is determined by who you are in secret, long-term, under pressure. As you commit to walking in the light of open confession (1 John 1:9), you will cultivate true inner beauty and holiness.

Listen, dear reader: It's never too late to be restored to

moral uprightness! Do not be discouraged with past failures. Commit yourself today to following Job's example. Repent quickly and thoroughly of all sin, and you will discover the honor that that kind of humility carries (1 Peter 5:5-6).

11. Be ethical in business practices (31:38-40).

"If my land cries out against me, and its furrows weep together; if I have eaten its fruit without money, or caused its owners to lose their lives; then let thistles grow instead of wheat, and weeds instead of barley." The words of Job are ended (31:38-40).

Job is declaring that he had not exploited or withheld wages from his servants and employees. He ends his monologue by addressing with full force the deceptive practices that pervade so much of the business community—the exploitation and oppression of laborers, using fraud and violence for self-advantage. These evil practices will be extremely repulsive to the endtime bride.

How you handle your business affairs is intensely important to God. Do you defraud workmen of their due wages? Do you confiscate goods from others? Is your leadership style tyrannical? Do you cheat on your taxes?

Above all, the endtime bride will carry a great passion for justice. She is waiting with trembling for the Judge of the whole earth to return that He might establish righteousness and retribution for all peoples.

There will be great financial blessing coming to the endtime bride—for the purpose of garnering the harvest—but it will be critically important that like Job, she be able to say that everything she gained was through honest means.

When A Holy Man Prays

There is not a more powerful combination on earth than these two ingredients: holiness and prayer. It's like putting gasoline and fire together. Mix holiness with prayer, and you've got combustion! It's a combination that changes earth and moves heaven.

The Bible testifies, "The effective, fervent *prayer of a righteous man* avails much" (James 5:16). Here's a simple formula for that verse:

$$purity + prayer = power$$

The glorious outcome of Job's story is almost inevitable because it's the story of a holy man who gives himself to prayer. When a man of holiness prays, his prayers are heard! Just as compromise hinders prayers (1 Peter 3:7), purity grants the confidence that God hears.

The Crucial Nature Of Moral Integrity

It is absolutely essential that we maintain our moral purity in the last hour. The battles will be intense and the pricetag of compromise high, but the rewards of purity will be lavishly rich.

Jesus said of Himself, "the ruler of this world is coming, and he has nothing in Me" (John 14:30). Jesus was saying that because of His moral purity, Satan could find no foothold in His life. There were no sinful handles in Jesus' heart that Satan could grab and manipulate. When we compromise ourselves morally, we grant Satan the legal right to establish a toehold of influence in that area. Once he has that access, he will manipulate it and work it, vying for even greater influence in our lives. Whenever there is darkness within our hearts, the prince of darkness has legal right to rule that area of darkness.

This truth is illustrated graphically within the small circle of Jesus' twelve disciples. Jesus has two general categories of disciples, represented in the lives of Judas Iscariot and Peter.

First, there's the Judas disciple who allows an ongoing pattern of moral compromise to continue unchecked in his life. The moral compromise of this disciple makes him openly vulnerable to Satan's schemes. Just as Satan was able to enter Judas in the end and use him like a pawn (John 13:26-30), Satan is able to yank this kind of disciple around at will, even drawing him to his destruction. Judas represents the disciple who gives Satan the legal right to rule in an area of his heart.

Then there's the Peter disciple. This disciple has established boundaries of moral purity around his life; he has formed walls of moral standards that he is committed to maintaining. For Satan to touch this kind of disciple, he has to ask first. "And the Lord said, 'Simon, Simon! Indeed, Satan has asked for you, that he may sift you as wheat. But I have prayed for you, that your faith should not fail; and when you have returned to Me, strengthen your brethren" (Luke 22:31-32).

Through personal purity, Peter had denied Satan the ability to gain any legal access to his life. Therefore, Satan had to get God's permission to touch Peter. The same was true of Job. There was no area of darkness in Job's life that Satan could exploit. Job was immune from Satan's manipulations because of his holiness and reverent fear (Job 1:8). Therefore, Satan had to get special permission from God to touch Job.

When Satan asks to sift you, and the Father gives him permission, notice these truths about that scenario:

- The Father sets the boundaries of how far Satan can take the sifting. The book of Job illustrates that when sifting a godly man, Satan can go so far and no further. He could touch Job's health but he couldn't take his life.

- Jesus is praying for you, "that your faith should not fail" (Luke 22:32).
- God has a purpose in it. Satan's agenda is to get you mad at God, to get you disoriented, to discourage your soul unto quitting. But God's agenda is that you persevere and come through, that you be changed in the process, and afterwards that you "strengthen your brethren" (Luke 22:32).

Satan will ask for permission to sift you because he has successfully engineered many casualties over the centuries. He has been able to discourage enough saints to the point of quitting that he's willing to take a gamble on your life. He thinks he can bring you down too. But you've got Jesus praying for you, and if you'll respond with grace in your heart, you will come through the crucible forever changed.

Satan becomes extremely nervous when he sees a saint holding to his moral purity and continuing to walk with righteous standards in the midst of the sifting. He knows that if the saint comes through the sifting successfully, he will become an even more effective servant for the cause of Christ.

Don't allow the final throes of his defeat to overwhelm you. *Guard your purity, hold to your virtues, continue to abound in good works, care for the poor and needy, and you will emerge from the crucible changed—truly a dangerous weapon in the hand of God!*

15

How God Changed
Job's Fathering Paradigm

When we look at Job at the beginning of the book, we find a man who was upright, holy, and blameless. But we also find a man who was deeply frustrated. He was frustrated at his inability to impart his passion for God on to his kids.

Job was holy, but he wasn't a real effective father. His first ten children were party animals (1:4-5). They were taking the financial blessing that had come to their father because of his godliness and were squandering it in a self-indulgent manner. They were not properly stewarding the blessing inherited from their father.

Job was personally blameless, but he couldn't impart his faith to his children. It almost seems like a contradiction, and yet it's a very common syndrome even today.

The book of Job tells the story of what happened when God decided to visit Job and transform his fathering paradigm—i.e., Job's formulated framework and automatic assumptions that drove and directed his mode and style of fathering.

Some people can see only *punishment* in God's disciplining hand. While there is an element of punishment in much of God's discipline, it's not always the prime element at work. Sometimes God's discipline is actually *promotion*. God didn't visit Job because of something he did wrong, but because of something he did right. Job's chastening wasn't a punishment for sin; it was the means whereby God was promoting Job because of his faithfulness.

Someone once asked me, "Can you find a God of mercy in the book of Job?" My answer is, absolutely! God could have said to Job, "Have your ten wayward children; have your crotchety wife; have your safe little world." God could have left Job alone. But He loved Job too much. It was the mercy of God that visited Job, to bring him to a higher place. God does not enjoy the process of inflicting pain upon our lives in order to draw us higher ("For He does not afflict willingly," Lamentations 3:33), but He knows it's the only way.

Job's Request

"I am one mocked by his friends, who called on God, and He answered him" (12:4). Job is telling us that his calamity came in answer to a prayer he offered. Job seems to be saying, "I asked God for something, and He answered my request. Now my friends mock me."

So the big question is, What did Job ask for?

It's clear he asked for *something*, but there's no way to prove what it was he asked for. However, I would like to make an "educated guess."

I think Job's prayer request related to his children. It's true that Job was a blameless man, but he was also a frustrated man. He was frustrated at the spiritual apathy of his ten children. It seemed that no matter how conscientiously he modeled godliness for them, they showed little interest in pursuing God like their father did. In fact, it appears that they felt their father's attentiveness placed them in a category of spiritual immunity. They were deceived into thinking that their father's sacrifices on their behalf exempted them from the consequences of their spiritual laziness.

Job was frustrated with his inability to ignite his children with his own passion for God. He was losing his kids to a self-indulgent lifestyle, and he felt helpless to do anything about it. Job was doing everything he knew to do as a parent, but it wasn't enough. The truth is, when it comes to raising kids, our best is never enough. We need God's divine help and intervention in our homes.

I am suggesting his prayer request sounded something like this: "God, what will it take to reach my kids? I pray that You would do whatever You need to do in me, to enable me to lead them into a passionate pursuit of God. Change me, Lord. Make me into a spiritual father. Bring me to a higher dimension in You."

The evidence is that this prayer pleased the Lord. It's as though God said, "Here, let me help. I will renew your wineskin. I will change the very fabric of your being, and you will become a true spiritual father."

The Meaning Of Job's Name

I was baffled by the multiple meanings given for Job's name. The Zondervan Pictorial Encyclopedia of the Bible said that Job's name could mean, "Where is my father?" or "No father." It then went on to say, "Either form might suggest an orphan or illegitimacy."

Clarke's Commentary (Volume III, p.23) said that Job means "Sorrowful" or "He that weeps."

Smith's Dictionary of the Bible (p. 1400) says Job means "Afflicted."

The Interpreter's Dictionary of the Bible (Volume 2, p. 911) connects the name Job with the Hebrew word for "enemy," thus suggesting that his name is associated with the idea of "Enmity" or "Hostility." The Interpreter's Dictionary was most helpful in terms of explaining the wide variety of meanings for Job's name. It's based upon the language being used. When using the Hebrew name for Job (ëiyyobh), it connects with "enemy" (ëoyebh). When studying the Arabic root of Job, it can mean "Penitent one" or "Sorrowful." The name Job also appears in Akkadian documents of the 2nd century B.C., and is explained by W. F. Albright as meaning "Where is (my) Father?"

Therefore, we can't be dogmatic with any one meaning of Job's name. However, I'm fascinated with the Akkadian connection—that Job's name means "Where is my father?" If Job didn't have a proper fathering model himself (a deficiency that plagues our world today), perhaps that would explain in part his apparent lack of knowing how to father his own children.

Renewing Job's Wineskin

To bring Job to a higher place, God had to revolutionize his fathering paradigm—his working framework of who a father is and what he does. God had to change Job in the essence of his being and personhood. This kind of radical personal transformation happens only in the crucible of intense heat and pressure. Nothing else can cause such dramatic change in the very nature of one's being. This wasn't simply a lesson that Job needed to learn; it was a life-changing experience that had to be branded into his soul through the training of God's discipline (Hebrews 12:11).

To use another metaphor for the same process, God was renewing Job's wineskin. To explain that metaphor, here's a quick summary of the winemaking process using a wineskin.

The new wine is placed into an animal skin that is shaped into the form of a container and then sewn closed and sealed tightly. As the wine ferments, it undergoes a vigorous chemical reaction, forcing the wineskin to stretch from the pressure of the expanding gases within. As the wine ages, the chemical reactions taper off, and the skin calcifies and hardens. After pouring off the aged wine, if you fill the hardened wineskin with new wine and seal it back up, the stiff wineskin will not be able to flex with the new wine as the expanding gases develop. The old wineskin will end up bursting from the violence of the chemical reactions within and will spill the contents. Jesus talked about this: "And no one puts new wine into old wineskins; or else the new wine bursts the wineskins, the wine is spilled, and the wineskins are ruined. But new wine must be put into new wineskins" (Mark 2:22).

You can do one of two things with an old wineskin: you can either discard it, or you can recondition it. To recondition an old wineskin so that it again becomes soft, supple, and flexible, is a very arduous task. Often it's easier to simply discard the thing. But sometimes God comes to an old wineskin and chooses it for new wine.

God chose Job for new wine, but He had to totally recondition his wineskin first. Otherwise, Job would have never been able to handle the new thing God wanted to do with him.

The processes of God in preparing an old wineskin for new wine are stringent and extremely intense. I'm made to understand that to prepare an old wineskin for new wine includes violent processes such as rubbing oil vehemently into the wineskin, rolling and stretching the skin vigorously, and placing it on the ground and pounding on it. After a little bit of that, we think we've had enough, but God knows we still need more pounding. We discover through Jonah's life that three days in the deep was not enough to change his wineskin. It will require more than a quick process to transform the old wineskin into a new readiness.

In one place the psalmist said, "For I have become like a wineskin in smoke, yet I do not forget Your statutes" (Psalm 119:83). Smoke will ruin a wineskin, for it will imbue and distort the flavor of the wine. My personal interpretation of Psalm 119:83 is that the writer is having his wineskin reconditioned by God, and he is feeling the painful intensity of the renewing process. In the immediacy of his distress, he feels like God is ruining him. (When God is renewing your wineskin, you will feel like the dealing is too hard and that you will not recover.) But despite his cry over the intensity of the discipline, the psalmist has the right response—he clings to God's word.

As God reworked Job's wineskin, he responded almost instinctively with fasting (6:6-7; 23:12). Fasting is one of the violent responses that you must employ if your old wineskin is being renewed by God. When Jesus taught about old wineskins and new wineskins, he was talking about fasting (see the context of Mark 2:22). To cooperate with God's purposes, fasting will be a necessary element if you are to come through successfully. I am not talking about fasting in the dutiful sense as the Pharisees practised it, but fasting as an act of mourning and humbling oneself before God, and as a way of intensifying one's pursuit of God.

How God Renewed Job's Wineskin

I will take some considerable time now to describe some of the forces at work in Job's life in order to delineate clearly the specific methods God used to renew Job's wineskin and transform his fathering paradigm. These are not mentioned in any particular order, but together they describe the nature of Job's crucible. It is my hope that these descriptions will enable you to understand, in part, the dealings of God in your own life.

1. The Pain Of Grief

Job's grief over his losses was incalculable. He cried, **"Oh, that my grief were fully weighed, and my calamity laid with it on the scales!"** (6:2) Job took a big-time hit in all three of the major areas of our lives: family relationships, finances, and physical health. If you are hit hard in just one of those three areas it's enough to put you into orbit. But Job suffered simultaneous losses in all three areas, and his sudden grief seemed unbearable.

It's very easy to judge someone who is in grief, especially if you've never experienced it yourself. Once you've experienced it, you'll never judge someone else's grief again. It's all too easy to stand from an aloof distance and criticize the depth and duration of someone's grief over a loss. It's easy to think, "Snap out of it already!" Until you've experienced a major loss in one of these three major areas, it's virtually impossible for you to appreciate or empathize with Job's grief.

Grief is the natural emotion we feel when we experience loss. Grief is most often associated with the death of a loved one, but in fact it happens in a multitude of ways: e.g., the loss of a job, of a friendship, of a bodily function, of a home, of financial security, of social status, of a marriage, of a ministry function, etc. Many times we don't label the fact that we're grieving until we're quite a ways into it. Then we realize, "I'm in grief! That's what I've been carrying! I've suffered a terrible loss, and I'm grieving that loss."

Those who don't understand your grief will try to fix it. They will search for ways to help you end your grief, but they don't realize that the grieving process is a gift from God, a necessary element in processing what has happened to you.

Jesus said that those who grieve are more blessed than those who laugh (Luke 6:21, 25). When you experience a loss, the best and most blessed thing you can do is mourn over that loss. We can pray, "I love You, Lord. I'm not mad at You, God. But my heart is very heavy because I feel the pain of my loss so intensely. I worship You, Almighty God, but I'm hurting." Or in the words of Job, **"The LORD gave, and the LORD has taken away; blessed be the name of the LORD" (1:21).**

I have nothing but respect for the intensity of Job's grief and how he handled it. He had no Scripture; he had no one speaking prophetic words of encouragement to him; to the contrary, all he got from his wife and friends were words of discouragement. And yet he still worshiped! Impressive, indeed.

Grief was one of the most fundamental and necessary elements at work in Job's soul to renew his wineskin.

2. The Pain Of Perplexity

Job and his three friends try to figure out why this calamity has happened to him. Although he's not totally sure, Job concludes that it must be God who has done this thing, for he says, **"If it is not He, who else could it be?"** (9:24). What a grueling question! Job is expressing his perplexity—if God hasn't done this to him, who has?

Job struggled frantically to discern the source of his calamity. It was a tornado-like wind that caused the house to fall upon Job's ten children (1:19). The Scriptures say, "[God] brings the wind out of His treasuries" (Psalm 135:7). So Job must have wondered, if it's God who controls the winds, how could Satan stir up a tornado? Was the tornado from God or Satan? And if God sent the tornado, then how is it that God would kill his children? It *must* have been Satan who killed his children—but how could Satan have that kind of authority over Job's family? These kinds of questions echoed and ricochetted incessantly in Job's mind with no satisfactory solution. He was in the grip of great perplexity.

When you've been traumatized by loss, your first instinct is to try to discern what has caused the loss. So you ask God, "Is this You, Lord, or is this the devil?"

The answer comes back, "Yes."

Well, if God had done this thing, you would know how to respond; or if Satan had done this thing, you would know what to do. The Scripture says, "Submit to God. Resist the devil" (James 4:7). If it's God, you submit; if it's the devil, you resist. But what do you do when you ask if it's God or the devil, and the answer comes back, "Yes"?

You don't want to submit to it because it might be the devil; and you don't want to resist it because it might be God. You don't know what to do! So you do nothing—

except stand there and cry. You cry out to God for grace, but you're not sure whether you're responding right or not.

Job had the hand of God on him, the hand of Satan on him, and the hand of man on him. Poor Job didn't know up from down! He was doing his best, but he couldn't discern where the shrapnel was coming from.

When God baptizes you with perplexity, He intentionally withholds light from your understanding. The perplexity has within itself unusual abilities to season the soul and excavate the heart. Herein is the power of perplexity. Perplexity is an absolutely essential part of the process. Job had no idea what was happening to him—until it was all over. If he had known about the heavenly wager going on over his life, he would have never emerged from the crucible with the quality of character which the perplexity was able to produce.

It's when we don't understand "why" that the quality of our love is assayed, tested, and purified.

The Bible records several instances where God's purposes and Satan's activities blur together in an indistinguishable manner. In one case it says, "But the Spirit of the LORD departed from Saul, and a distressing spirit from the LORD troubled him. And Saul's servants said to him, 'Surely, a distressing spirit from God is troubling you" (1 Samuel 16:14-15). So was the distressing spirit (or as some translations put it, the evil spirit) a demon deployed by God or a heavenly angel? How can something evil come from God? Or how about 1 Kings 22:23, "Therefore look! The LORD has put a lying spirit in the mouth of all these prophets of yours, and the LORD has declared disaster against you." How is it that a lying spirit can come from God?

An even better example of the demonic and heavenly realms being strangely indistinguishable is found in the account of David commanding that the people of Israel be numbered. The story is told two different ways in two portions of Scripture:

- 2 Samuel 24:1, Again the anger of the LORD was aroused against Israel, and He moved David against them to say, "Go, number Israel and Judah."
- 1 Chronicles 21:1, Now Satan stood up against Israel, and moved David to number Israel.

2 Samuel says that God moved David to number the people; 1 Chronicles says that Satan moved David to number the people. So who did it, God or Satan? The answer is, "Yes." Sometimes the hand of God and the hand of Satan are almost impossible for us to differentiate given our limited human perspective.

In the case of Job, God had picked the fight, and Satan was being used as the tool. But Job didn't know that! Job didn't know about chapters 1 and 2 until after the whole ordeal was over! So right now he's in the vortex of the maelstrom, and he doesn't know what to do.

Job's perplexity serves as a sign for the end times. The Spirit of God testifies that perplexity will be one of the great issues men will face in the last days. Jesus said, "And there will be signs in the sun, in the moon, and in the stars; and on the earth distress of nations, with perplexity, the sea and the waves roaring" (Luke 21:25). Jesus warned that in the last days men will be utterly baffled at the things that will be happening in their lives. Be watchful: perplexity is on the increase all around us.

It's not just unbelievers that will be perplexed. The saints will be also. The book of Revelation describes a number of last-day occurrences which will be instigated by both the hand of God and the hand of Satan. Even the saints will be unable at times to discern what is of God and what is of Satan. Here are two examples from Revelation:

So I looked, and behold, a pale horse. And the name of him who sat on it was Death, and Hades followed with him. And power was given to them over a fourth of the earth, to kill with sword, with hunger, with death, and by the beasts of the earth (Revelation 6:8).

The context of this verse is John's describing how he is caught up to the throne of God and how the heavens are opened to him. He sees four different horses ride forth, each apparently originating from heaven. But the rider on this horse is named Death, and Hades follows with him. So this thing appears to originate in heaven, but it carries hell's hordes in its train. So is this coming from God or from Satan? As these woes hit the earth in our day, it is almost impossible to totally discern the source.

Then I heard a loud voice from the temple saying to the seven angels, "Go and pour out the bowls of the wrath of God on the earth"...8 Then the fourth angel poured out his bowl on the sun, and power was given to him to scorch men with fire. 9 And men were scorched with great heat, and they blasphemed the name of God who has power over these plagues; and they did not repent and give Him glory. 10 Then the fifth angel poured out his bowl on the throne of the beast, and his kingdom became full of darkness; and they gnawed their tongues because of the pain. 11 They blasphemed the God of heaven because of their pains and their sores, and did not repent of their deeds...21 And great hail from heaven fell upon men, each hailstone about the weight of a talent. Men blasphemed God because of the plague of the hail, since that plague was exceedingly great (Revelation 16:1, 8-11, 21).

Three times in Revelation 16 it says that men blasphemed God because of their plagues. The big issue for Job, when he was plagued, was whether he would blaspheme God. "Curse God and die!" prodded his wife (2:9). If Job had cursed God, he would never have entered into his greater inheritance. But in the end times, men will forsake their integrity and curse God because of their pain. Instead of qualifying for a higher place, they will go to perdition bitter against God.

Notice in Revelation 16:11, quoted above, that men will blaspheme God because of their sores. The first shall be last. The first plague will be the last plague. Job's sores will again appear on men's flesh. Thus, Job is a prophetic sign to the endtime generation of the intensity of the plagues that will visit mankind, and he will appear in judgment on the last day as a witness against all those who choose to blaspheme God instead of blessing His name.

But again, my primary reason for quoting this passage in Revelation 16 is to show the blurring of the lines that distinguish the hand of God from the hand of Satan. The bowls originate from heaven, and they are poured out by angels at God's command, but the manifestations of their contents are more generally ascribed in our day to the works of the devil: disease, scorching fire, darkness, plagues, sores, pain, the release of froglike demons from the mouth of the dragon, earthquakes, and deadly hailstones. When God visits the earth with these plagues, great perplexity will grip the hearts of men as they struggle to discern what is from God and what is from Satan.

God used perplexity to recondition Job's wineskin. And He will again use the power of perplexity in the last days to totally refashion His endtime servants, to change their fathering paradigm, and to accelerate their maturity and passion for Jesus in the face of expanding evil.

3. The Pain Of Reproach

"These ten times you have reproached me; you are not ashamed that you have wronged me" (19:3).

Job felt the sting of the stigma associated with his crucible. The trauma had put his every nerve on full alert, and now he felt every nuance of the raised eyebrows, the critical words, the skeptical attitudes, and the questioning looks that came his way because of God's hand on his life.

When you've been wounded by God, you walk around with the constant premonition that people are looking at the back of your head and talking about you. "I wonder what she did wrong." Sometimes you're just imagining what they're saying, and sometimes it's more than just your imagination—people really are looking and wondering. And the reason you know they're talking about you is because you talked about them when it happened to them. But after your season in the fire, you won't judge others so rashly again.

Here's the reason they reproached Job: the means whereby God promotes His choicest servants is the same means by which He punishes the disobedient. To the undiscerning, God's hand of punishment looks identical to His hand of promotion. The afflictions and crisis and imprisonment look the same for both. God has purposed that this sameness confuse the undiscerning, causing them to misdiagnose what He is doing in Job. The reproach that stems from their misdiagnosis is a critical element in the reworking of Job's wineskin.

God purposely orchestrates the thing so others don't know what's happening to you. Job said of his friends, **"For You have hidden their heart from understanding; therefore You will not exalt them"** (17:4). In a similar way, your friends conclude in their own minds that you've blown it and that God is displeased with you. This validates their decision to remove you from ministry or administer some sort of church discipline. They might say, "We love you very much, but as long as you're working through these issues in your life, we think it's best for your sake that you take a rest from ministry." And they actually might be right; you probably need to put away all distractions and spend more focused time at Christ's feet. But the removal can also be totally invalid.

This can sometimes be what it means to share in "the reproach of Christ" (Hebrews 11:26). Even as the religious leaders thought Jesus was abandoned by God, today's leaders may think that God is greatly displeased with you, too. *But you cannot have the reward without the reproach* (Hebrews 11:26).

One of the strategic issues God is surfacing in this matter of reproach is how all of us tend to drink in the praise of man. (I write about this at length in my booklet, "Dealing With The Rejection And Praise Of Man.") God wants to dislodge you from your fleshly need to garner the approval of people. In order to perfect this work in your heart, He will cause those you love and respect to reject and reproach you.

Some of you are presently feeling the same kind of reproach from your friends that Job felt from his friends. The fire of this reproach is an essential instrument in God's hand to prepare your wineskin for greater works.

4. The Pain Of Shattered Vision

Job lamented, **"My purposes are broken off"** (17:11). Job is saying that every visionary goal he had for his life was suddenly decimated. All his life goals were destroyed, and now he was incapable of formulating fresh vision for the future.

I remember the time my staff pastors came to me as their senior pastor and asked me what my vision was for our local church. My response was, "I don't have a vision for our church. My vision is to survive today." Imagine having to live with that kind of visionary leadership!

When God reduces a once-visionary leader to a moment-by-moment survival mode, the pain is incredible. One of the purposes of God in this "vision blackout" is to re-train His servant's paradigm of what it means to provide visionary leadership.

In this place of dependence upon God, the broken leader begins to realize how many of his past visionary goals were not received from the place of intimacy with Jesus but were rather the result of his own creativity or the product of group-session brainstorming. The shock of that realization causes him to rethink his leadership style. He begins to see that he will be much more fruitful in the harvest if he will wait until he hears from God rather than pressing forward with his own ideas.

It's much easier to be creative than obedient. Because sometimes God waits longer than we like. In the time it takes to hear from God, we could have had ten incredibly creative ideas up and running! *But the balancing truth is this: one idea received from the throne will accomplish more than all of our own ideas combined.* Besides, implementing our own creative ideas is hard work; implementing God-inspired ideas is invigorating because they are empowered by abundant grace.

When I looked back in retrospect over the years during which my only vision was daily survival, I was fascinated with this observation: being reduced to listening daily to God's voice and simply obeying Him produced a greater harvest for the kingdom than the labors of some who were articulating great futuristic goals. The place of broken purpose can become the place of reborn purpose.

When Job tells of his purposes being broken off, he is venting a great cry of pain. But he is also interpreting for us a vital element in the remaking of our wineskins. The process is excruciating, but God's intent is that His servant emerge from the crucible with the primary purpose of hearing in the place of intimacy with God, and then doing what He says. This is preparing the servant for true spiritual fatherhood, and this kind of fathering model carries the greatest potential for sheer adventure with God!

5. The Pain Of Theological Crisis

"I was at ease, but He has shattered me; He also has taken me by my neck, and shaken me to pieces; He has set me up for His target, His archers surround me. He pierces my heart and does not pity; He pours out my gall on the ground. He

breaks me with wound upon wound; He runs at me like a warrior. I have sewn sackcloth over my skin, and laid my head in the dust. My face is flushed from weeping, and on my eyelids is the shadow of death; although no violence is in my hands, and my prayer is pure" (16:12-17).

Although there is no violence in Job's hands, and his prayer is pure, yet God has set him up as a target for wounding. Job does not understand this. He is in a theological crisis right now because everything he ever believed has collapsed under him and he's having to rethink every presupposition he ever believed about God. The great theological question is, "Why would God do this to me when I'm walking in obedience, loving Him, doing His will, and keeping myself pure and morally blameless?"

Job no doubt shared the same theological position of his three friends, until he entered his own inexplicable crisis. Now, he can no longer hold to the standard theology that he had once believed. I can imagine Job saying to his friends, "Listen, guys, I've been the teacher of systematic theology. I know your arguments inside out because I once believed and taught them. But I can no longer embrace your simplistic answers. God has unravelled my theology. And although I don't know what to believe, I know that I no longer believe your standardized theology."

Job had encountered the God who fries your theological circuits. Just when you get comfortable with your understanding of God, He comes along and devastates your most foundational constructs of who He is.

There are few things more painful than having an experience in God for which you have no scriptural understanding. You think to yourself, "If this is in the Bible, I don't know where it is." What God is doing here is dismantling your theology in order to introduce Himself to you all over again. The Bible gives one clear quality of spiritual fathers: "I write to you, fathers, because you have known Him who is from the beginning" (1 John 2:13). Spiritual fathers have truly come to know God—God in His eternity, God in His sovereignty, God who is the Beginning and the End.

It's one thing to learn about God through second-hand information, but Job had come to know God personally through a first-hand encounter with Him. This was an essential element in reshaping Job's fathering paradigm. Now he would father as a man with a profoundly personal history in God. Job no longer constricted God to a set of principles for He knew God in His boundless personhood.

Some people act as though God is limited to the Bible. "If it's not in the Bible, He can't do it." Oh, really? God didn't write the Bible for Himself but for us. The Everlasting One will never be limited by any external constraint, not even the Bible. God will never act in an anti-biblical manner, but He is always free to act in a supra-biblical ("beyond the Bible") way—which will always be consistent with His ways recorded in the Bible. Spiritual fathers are those who have come to know God in His boundless, sovereign, eternal glory and splendor (1 John 2:13). Spiritual fathers have had to seek God's face with an unusual abandonment because of their theological crisis—and as a result have gone through a spiritual metamorphosis whereby they are immersed into the knowledge of God in a new and living way.

There are no more moving words in the entire book than Job's concluding utterance: **"I have heard of You by the hearing of the ear, but now my eye sees You. Therefore I abhor myself, and repent in dust and ashes"** (42:5-6). O the revolutionizing paradigm shift that comes from beholding God! Nothing remains the same when you see God! Job was eternally changed by this ineffable encounter with God Himself. *On the other side of the theological crisis is a whole new revelation of God.*

6. The Pain Of Disarmament

Job cries out, **"He has loosed my bowstring and afflicted me"** (30:11). The bowstring is that part of the bow into which the arrow is fitted; then the archer pulls back the bowstring and deploys the arrow. Thus the bowstring represents the ability to draw back and thrust forward; it represents the ability to defend from attack, and to move forward in offensive warfare.

When your bowstring is loosed, you have no ability to fight. At one point I said to the Lord, "Lord, if this an attack of the devil, I'm lunch," because I was absolutely powerless to defend myself from spiritual attack. I could only throw myself upon the mercy of God and fasten my love upon Him.

There are many books, tapes, and conferences on spiritual warfare today, and yet few discuss the reality of how to walk through the maze of spiritual warfare with a loosed bowstring. When you've been unstrung, it is incredibly painful to listen to the exhortations of others in the body of Christ as they urge you to rise up and fight. They do not understand or believe that you are incapable of defending yourself right now. Not everyone has experienced that place of absolute brokenness and weakness. **"But now He has worn me out"** (16:7).

Here's what God is up to in this thing, at least in part: "He breaks [your] bow" (Psalm 46:9) because of your ineffectiveness and ineptitude in spiritual warfare. You thought you were hitting the mark pretty well, but He begins to reveal that you were actually "turned aside like a deceitful bow" (Psalm 78:57). He shows you how the arrows that you've launched in ministry have been further off center than you realized. *He intends to heal your weapon, and once healed you will hit the mark with much greater accuracy.*

In Zechariah 9:11-13, the Lord shows how He incarcerates His people in a prison of hope in order to bring them out as a mighty bow in His hand that He can deploy.

The context goes on to call the Messiah God's "battle bow" (Zechariah 10:4).

Jesus recognized that He was like a bow in God's hand when He said, "He who speaks from himself seeks his own glory; but He who seeks the glory of the One who sent Him is true, and no unrighteousness is in Him" (John 7:18). The word "true" is an archer's term. When an arrow flies true to the mark, it hits the mark dead center. So Jesus was saying, "The one who speaks a message that originates in his own heart is speaking in such a way as to seek glory for himself from other people." When we preach the gospel with a subtle inner desire to impress others we will not be "true"—our ministry will not hit the mark dead center.

"But He who seeks the glory of the One who sent Him is true." Only the one who seeks to glorify God (really and truly) is able to be "true" to the mark. *When we carry even the slightest desire to impress those around us, arrows that we deploy in ministry may start out right, but then in transit they veer away from the mark.* It's because they're not deployed by a "true" bow.

Jesus was dealing here with the most fundamental issue that contributes to inaccuracy in warfare: the subtle desire to look good before people. God will disarm you in order to deal most forcefully in your heart regarding the issue of receiving the praise of man. Once healed, you will become dangerously precise in spiritual warfare.

When God loosed Job's bowstring, He began to revolutionize Job's fathering paradigm. By the time he emerged from the crucible, Job was much more accurate in spiritual warfare. The spiritual attacks on his household still came but he was equipped to do warfare on behalf of his children in a much more effectual way, helping them to walk toward their highest inheritance.

7. The Pain Of God-Forsakenness

Job's lament says it all: **"Look, I go forward, but He is not there, and backward, but I cannot perceive Him; when He works on the left hand, I cannot behold Him; when He turns to the right hand, I cannot see Him"** (23:8-9).

Job no longer has any awareness of God's presence in His life. God seems to be a thousand miles away and seems to refuse to hear Job's cries. In a technical sense we know that God never leaves us nor forsakes us (Hebrews 13:5), but when we're in the vortex of the emotional isolation of this thing, it becomes very challenging to believe that God is indeed with us.

The pain of this seeming abandonment by God is exacerbated by the fact that the sweetest joy in your life was the blessed awareness of His presence and affection in your life. You have known the kisses of His mouth (His living words); you have drunk deeply of the new wine of His embrace. You have known the addictive delight of being filled with the Holy Spirit—drinking at the fountain of God, releasing the flow of heavenly language, basking in the glory of the only thing that satisfies the deepest longing of the human spirit. But now your awareness of His presence has lifted (even though He is still there), and you don't know why.

In the past, you learned that His presence lifted because of your disobedience. When you repented, that sense of His presence was sweetly restored. Now, you can't repent yourself back into His arms. No matter what you say, or how you pray, nothing changes. The heavens are brass; your prayers remain unanswered. When the awareness of God's presence lifts, you will be tempted to give up trying to pray.

When God lifts the awareness that He's hearing our prayers, some people get offended at God. Actually, all the great men of the Bible were given opportunity to be offended at Him—Abraham, Job, David, John the Baptist, and many others. Before we qualify for the greatest service and greatest fruitfulness, we must pass the offence test.

He's asking, "Do you love Me, even if you can't feel My presence?" *He offends the mind to reveal the heart.*

One of the purposes of the test of abandonment—called "the silence of God"—is to determine whether you serve God only because of the good rewards of His Holy Spirit. Do you serve Him because He satisfies your inner longings and answers your prayers? Or do you serve Him because you love Him for who He is, even if He never again does a solitary thing for you?

The dryness of this spiritual season is a powerful factor in the remaking of Job's wineskin.

8. The Pain Of Isolation

Job refers repeatedly to his loneliness: **"He has removed my brothers far from me, and my acquaintances are completely estranged from me. My relatives have failed, and my close friends have forgotten me"** (19:13-14). **"I am a brother of jackals, and a companion of ostriches"** (30:29).

God has made us social creatures. By His design, we gain emotional fulfillment and delight from our interaction with the circle of personal friends surrounding our lives. There are few things more important to us in life than enjoying and keeping the right friends.

But when you enter the Job crucible, most if not all of your friendships change. The resulting social isolation is agonizing. Some of your friends no longer understand you. Some of your family members pull away from you, or you from them. You begin to feel like you're suffering all by yourself, like you can no longer unload your heart to those you once trusted.

In the loneliness of your heart, you begin to cry out to God more than ever. And that's exactly what He was waiting for! His intention is that you not be distracted by socializing right now, but that you devote large chunks of time to the secret place. In that quiet place with God, you will begin to discover that it actually is possible to fulfill one's social needs in the prayer closet. God really is delightful to talk to! God will become the one who meets your social needs, thus liberating you to relate to everyone you know with total freedom.

God will separate you from the ones to which He will send you. It's only through the separation that they will be able to recognize the changed wineskin of your life. You may very possibly return to those friends later, but if you do, the nature of the relationship will be permanently different.

It was the separation that enabled Job's family and friends to welcome him back into their lives on a totally new basis (see 42:11). Because of God's accelerated purposes in his life, he seemed to them to be a very different person. And he was!

9. The Pain Of Waiting

Job grits his teeth and says, **"All the days of my hard service I will wait, till my change comes"** (14:14). He is adamantly committed to waiting on God, until.

We have some songs that we sing in America about waiting on God. They are sweet songs with lilting tunes. But there's nothing sweet or lilty or singsongy about waiting on God.

Waiting on God is the hottest flame. It can be absolutely excruciating. When the heat is on, everyone is watching, your circumstances are crying out for immediate action, and all God says is wait. It doesn't get any hotter than that. Please don't make the song fun because waiting isn't fun.

You can't tell anyone that you're waiting on God. You go to work; everyone knows what's happening in your life, so they ask you what you're doing about it. You're tongue-tied. How do you tell those unbelievers that you're waiting on God? And you can't tell your mother-in-law. Your family is waiting for you to grow up and take responsibility for your life. But God won't let you take action; He's insisting that you wait on Him. This is pure heat and pressure.

The more I looked at this, the more I realized that all the greatest saints of the Bible had one common experience: they all had protracted seasons of waiting on God for the fulfillment of His Word. *Waiting is a critical element in bringing God's saints to the highest mountains of spiritual promotion.*

Waiting is essential if we are ever to step into God's time zone. His timing and ways are so radically different from ours (Isaiah 55:8-9), and we will never grow in our understanding of His ways without the enforced discipline of waiting. We will always be frustrated with God's timetable until we're immersed into the knowledge of His ways—and that enlargement of spiritual perspective is impossible without much waiting on God.

There is only one way to learn endurance and patience and that is through waiting. The first Old Testament book written (Job) is a treatise on waiting on God. Interestingly enough, the first New Testament book written begins with the very same theme. There is no way to prove beyond all doubt exactly which New Testament book was written first. However, most scholars agree, after carefully examining the evidence, that it was probably the book of James. With that in mind, look at the first words of the New Testament ever put on paper:

> *James, a bondservant of God and of the Lord Jesus Christ, to the twelve tribes which are scattered abroad: Greetings. My brethren, count it all joy when you fall into various trials, knowing that the testing of your faith produces patience. But let patience have its perfect work, that you may be perfect and complete, lacking nothing (James 1:1-4).*

The New Testament starts with the same theme as the Old Testament—how to endure patiently while being tested by various trials. Like Job, we "fall" into various trials. The righteous fall, sometimes seven times, but they rise each time (Proverbs 24:16). The testing produces patience (endurance), and patience is the thing that will make us perfect and complete, lacking nothing.

When God is really serious about doing a speedy work in a saint, He'll stop everything. All forward movement grinds to a halt. Because to do the quickest work, God waits. Everything stops, the flame gets turned on high, and the refining process is accelerated. Waiting is the hottest flame, but when embraced properly it becomes the catalyst to an accelerated learning curve. What would have normally taken ten years to accomplish in your heart will now be done in three.

Job's crucible was not measured in days or weeks, but in months (7:3; 29:2). It was necessary that the season be long enough in order to totally rework Job's wineskin and transform him into genuine spiritual fatherhood. As Job waited upon God, the thing that Satan intended to use to bring him down was the very thing God used to make him perfect!

10. The Pain Of The Terror Of The Lord

"Therefore I am terrified at His presence; when I consider this, I am afraid of Him. For God made my heart weak, and the Almighty terrifies me" (23:15-16).

The fear of the Lord, properly understood, is terrorizing. Job did not rightly fear God on his own. He needed help from God if he was to be baptized into the fear of the Lord.

When God touches your life and takes something away from you, you experience the terror of the Lord. He who touched this one little area of your life is capable of touching so much more. If His loving hand is this painful, what would His hand of judgment be like? One shudders to even consider it.

To be awakened to the fear of the Lord is thunderously painful. I have spoken with a couple saints who have had singularly outstanding visitations of God in His holiness, and the common denominator they articulate is an over-whelming fear of God. In the immediacy of God's holiness, they were painfully aware of their frailty and the unclean-ness of their hands. It's a fear that shook them to the core and was not expressed as a pleasant experience.

When some people teach the fear of the Lord, they di-lute its strength. They say, "Well, we really don't fear God, we just reverence Him." No, we really do fear Him!

Paul wrote of two realities which motivated him to reach out to the lost as Christ's ambassador. The following two portions are just three verses apart: "Knowing, therefore, the terror of the Lord, we persuade men" (2 Corinthians 5:11); "For the love of Christ compels us" (2 Corinthians 5:14).

Paul was motivated by both the terror of the Lord and the love of Christ. The terror of the Lord pushed him, the love of Christ pulled him. He *had* to preach the gospel! We will always lack motivation to touch the lost until we know both the terror of the Lord and the love of Christ. I personally feel that I woefully lack in both areas and constantly ask Him to fill me with the knowledge of His terror and His love.

When God terrorized Job, it revolutionized his wineskin. Job was awakened to a new dimension of the fear of the Lord—an essential element in equipping him to become an effective spiritual father.

11. The Pain Of Ruined Success

"You spoil my success" (30:22). Job was highly es-teemed in his day because of God's blessings in his life. God had made him successful in business so Job was un-commonly wealthy and influential. Then, it all disappeared in literally one day.

It is profoundly painful when God reverses what was a pattern of success and blessing in life. At one time you were perceived by some as being greatly blessed of God in your ministry; but then after God launched you into the paradigm shift, others began to perceive you as primarily responsible for the struggle and floundering of the ministry.

I have personally known the pain of having to resign from ministries that were meaningful to me. In the instance of one ministry responsibility I was outright called upon to resign, in other instances I could no longer fulfill the reasonable expectations of others. Slowly many things were stripped or fallen away. Eventually, I resigned the pastorate after thirteen fruitful years.

This scenario does not apply solely to ministry positions. It can involve a spoiling of ministry success, or financial success, or career success, or family success. Nothing gets our attention faster than ruined success.

God has His ways of exposing our selfish ambitions and our pride. We don't see it until He exposes it. In the heat of the crucible, suddenly we see the motivations of our hearts in stark reality. The revelation is stunning. "Lord, where did that come from??" The Lord says, "It was there all along. I'm using the fire to bring it to the surface so you can see it."

You can't repent of something you don't see. So God turns up the fire, brings a reversal in your succession of successes, and uses your "ministry recession" to reveal the true motives of the heart.

Sometimes your best is not enough. When God purposes to tenderize your spirit with spoiled success, you can do everything right but things will still unravel. When we watch our area of strength or expertise begin to crumble, our tendency is to recreate the scenario over and over in our minds, grasping to find a way we could have done things different or better.

You can work your fingers to the bone right now, but this ship is not going to turn around. Your best efforts will accomplish very little. God is spoiling your success. He is doing a number on your wineskin.

God was preparing Job for greater success than he had ever known, but in order to be prepared for the promotion Job needed the crushing of spoiled success. Through the crushing disappointment, God was equipping Job's wineskin to handle a season of new wine—success of a much higher dimension.

12.   The Pain Of Songlessness

Consider the agony of Job's soul as he writes, **"My harp is turned to mourning, and my flute to the voice of those who weep"** (30:31). God had displaced Job's joyful song and instead given him tears and weeping.

I identify with Job very personally on this point. At the time of this writing, it's been seven years since I've been able to sing. Singing was central to my life! I was a piano player and worship leader, and was frequently asked to lead worship for various events regionally and nationally. I will not even try to convey the emotional pain of being rendered without a song.

I will tell just one personal story in this connection. I remember standing in a praise service one time, when others around me were dancing and clapping and rejoicing, and all I could do was weep. I thought within myself, "Lord, this is real bad. I've written this book *(Exploring Worship)* which is being used literally around the world to teach your people on the sacrifice of praise. And now that calamity has hit my life, I can't even practice what I've preached. I have no sacrifice of praise; I simply cannot find it within me. There is something dreadfully wrong with this picture. Lord, why can't I praise you now, like I've taught others to do? Am I a hypocrite? I must be very displeasing to You right now."

Then the Lord directed my heart to Psalm 103:1, "Bless the LORD, O my soul; *and all that is within me,* bless His holy name!" I sensed the Lord asking me, "Bob, what is within you?" I responded, "Lord, all I've got are tears." He said, "Give Me what you've got."

God was going to restore Job's song, but in the meantime the songlessness was a powerful ingredient in reconditioning his soul, preparing his wineskin for something greater.

13. The Pain Of False Accusation

Eliphaz was the first of Job's friends to speak with Job, which would suggest he was possibly the closest of the three. He may have been Job's best friend. If so, that would have made Eliphaz's accusations all the more painful to Job.

Eliphaz had a mounting frustration in the book. He was not able to convince Job of his sin. Finally, after two unsuccessful attempts to build a case against Job, he began to fabricate charges. He figured Job must be guilty of something heinous, so he began to accuse Job of the sorts of things that would normally incur this kind of calamity from God. So he says to his good friend, **"For you have taken pledges from your brother for no reason, and stripped the naked of their clothing. You have not given the weary water to drink, and you have withheld bread from the hungry. But the mighty man possessed the land, and the honorable man dwelt in it. You have sent widows away empty, and the strength of the fatherless was crushed"** (22:6-10). But if anyone would know these things are all lies, surely it would be Eliphaz! His anger had so discolored his discernment that Eliphaz began to trump up false charges against his friend.

Elihu also brought false charges against Job: **"Oh, that Job were tried to the utmost, because his answers are like those of wicked men! For he adds rebellion to his sin; he claps his hands among us, and multiplies his words against God"** (34:36-37).

False accusations don't carry much weight until they begin to come from those who are closest to you. Then they suddenly become powerful catalysts for reworking your wineskin.

When the false accusations came, Job was able to guard his heart against a bitter spirit. He was able to see that the false accusations were part of God's disciplinary purpose in his life. That's why it wasn't difficult for him to pray for his friends at the end of the book (42:10). God used the specter of false accusation to bring Job into fatherhood.

We've been surveying the various ways God uses to renew our wineskin and to change our fathering paradigm. We have coined each one with the phrase, "The pain of..." Now, we'll look at our final consideration, the pain of constant transition.

14. The Pain Of Constant Transition

Job put it this way, **"Changes and war are ever with me"** (10:17). Job felt like he was in a warzone, with changes happening around his life with incessant regularity. As the popular saying goes, "Constant change is here to stay."

But Job wasn't simply talking about the normal changes that accompany everyday growth. Everybody meets up with changes of some degree literally every day, but that's not what Job was talking about.

Job was talking about the floorboards that support his footing—the foundational elements of life that give us a sense of emotional and mental equilibrium. He was saying, "The places where I can find solid footing are continually changing, so that I am constantly stumbling in my orientation to life and my sense of focus and direction." His scenery wouldn't stop changing, and the stress load from nonstop transitions was stripping his soul.

Job is being carried along right now by a river that is over his head. He cannot touch bottom. And the river is flowing at flood stage. He is being carried along in a current of constant change, and he can do nothing about the direction he's going. He has lost control.

Job doesn't understand yet what God is doing in him, but through these fourteen elements (and I'm sure there were others as well), God is changing the essence of his personhood. His motives are changing, his values are changing, his priorities are changing. His concept of spiritual parenting is being totally revamped. He will emerge in the end with an entirely new paradigm of fathering, enabling him to father a generation that will be radically different from his first ten children.

A Troubling Syndrome

There is a disturbing syndrome which surfaces often throughout the Old Testament stories: some of the godliest fathers raised the ungodliest sons. Some sad examples of this:

- The mighty prophet Samuel reared sons who were dishonest and greedy (1 Samuel 8:3-5).
- Three of King David's sons (Absalom, Adonijah, and Amnon) perished prematurely because of their lust, anger, and selfish ambition.
- Jehoshaphat was an upright king, but his son Jehoram was a brutal murderer who led the nation into idolatry (2 Chronicles 21:4-11).
- Hezekiah, the godly king who restored Temple worship to Judah, fathered Manasseh who was probably the most ungodly king to reign in Jerusalem.

It's worth mentioning, however, that the inverse of this syndrome is also true—that God, in His grace, also called forth some of His greatest saints from the pit of an ungodly upbringing. Men like Noah, Abraham, Jonathan, and Josiah are evidence to the grace of God—that He can redeem men to Himself from the worst of family backgrounds.

Nevertheless it remains true that many of the great spiritual leaders of the Bible struggled with the inability to impart their spirituality to their children.

God has always purposed that fathers raise up godly offspring. Malachi 2:15 explains that the reason God joins a married couple together is because "He seeks godly offspring." *God passionately desires that the spiritual heights attained by one generation become the platform from which the next generation springboards into even greater heights in God.*

Job struggled with the same syndrome, however. He couldn't ignite his children with his own passion for God. We are now approaching the very heartbeat of the book of Job, the central issue around which everything in the book turns.

The significance of Job's ordeal is seen in the difference between his first ten children and his second ten children. A comparison between the two sets of children illumines what the book is all about.

Job's first set of children were party animals. They were squandering the blessings of God in self-indulgence. They figured, "God likes Dad best. God listens to Dad. Dad will offer a sacrifice for us; he'll make sure we're all squared away with God. So party up!" Their problem, in a nutshell, was spiritual passivity.

Job's second set of children, however, were radically different. They were outstanding in spiritual beauty and caliber and integrity (see chapter 42). And the difference between the two sets of children was Job. God had changed the man. Job didn't have to try to be a better father; he was just being himself. But he was so radically changed by the crucible that he had emerged as a true spiritual father.

Job's story illustrates a powerful scriptural principle: *When God targets a generation, He starts by preparing the generation before.* To raise up a chosen generation, God prepares the fathers (and mothers).

Job's is not the only profile to illustrate this truth. This principle is also graphically portrayed in Jacob's encounter with God at Peniel. God met Jacob at Peniel in order to change his fathering paradigm. Let me explain.

Peniel

Peniel was the location where a heavenly Man appeared to Jacob and wrestled with him all night (Genesis 32:24-32).

As morning began to dawn, Jacob would not release his hold on the Man, so He touched Jacob in his hip. Jacob limped from that day forward. Jacob's limp represents God's mark on the man who has wrestled through the dark night of the soul and has come out changed. The Man also changed Jacob's name to Israel. But I want you to see that Peniel was not so much about Jacob as it was about Joseph.

Jacob's performance rating as a father was not very good. His first son Reuben lay with Jacob's concubine; his next two sons Simeon and Levi were hotheads. Their tempers caused them to murder an entire community of men. His fourth son Judah had a problem with prostitutes. And God said, "This thing is not going in the right direction. If you stay on this course, Jacob, I'll never get the Joseph that I need for My purposes. I'm going to change your walk." So God intercepted Jacob's life and renewed his wineskin.

Peniel changed Jacob dramatically. Because of his shrunken hip, he had to guard each step. If he took a careless turn, his bum leg could go out from under him, and he would end up on the ground. So now Jacob gingerly plotted every move. With every step as a father, he cried out to God for help and wisdom. We don't need fathers who know what they're doing; we need fathers who have been broken of their self-confidence and who have gained a profound tentativeness and dependence upon God for every move they make.

Secondly, Jacob's name was changed to Israel. "Jacob" means "Trickster" or "Deceiver," and Israel means "Prince With God." Jacob may have limped, but he did so with square shoulders. He lived under the personal awareness that God liked and favored him and that he was chosen for a unique blessing. He understood his weakness (the limp), but he also understood what God was making him to be, a Prince With God. Jacob's fathering paradigm was revolutionized.

The reason for Jacob's pain of Peniel was because God needed a Joseph. And to get a Joseph, God needed a father who could raise up a Joseph. So God visited Jacob. Josephs don't happen in a vacuum; they're fathered. Joseph's older brothers were fathered by Jacob, but Joseph was fathered by Israel. Now, Israel was able to implant a deposit of faith in his son that would enable Joseph to persevere through enslavement and imprisonment.

If Jacob had known unbroken blessing, he would not have been equipped to prepare Joseph for slavery and imprisonment. Jacob had Peniel; Joseph had prison. When trying to interpret his prison, Joseph could look back on his father's Peniel, and start to piece together a beginning understanding of the ways of God. This is one of the foremost qualities of spiritual fatherhood: *Spiritual fathers bequest to the next generation an example and pattern which enables the next generation to cooperate with the shaping processes of God.*

Endtime Preparation

God did in Job the same thing He did in Jacob at Peniel. He used Job's calamity to prepare him for a totally new dimension of spiritual fatherhood. At the beginning of the book, Job was an ineffective father. At the end of the book, he is effectively imparting a fantastic legacy to his children, catapulting them into their own exciting spiritual inheritance and walk with God.

Job's story is a living parable of how God will be working in the lives of His servants in the last hour. Job is a prophetic forerunner revealing the nature of God's endtime strategies to raise up spiritual fathers with great anointing and fruitfulness.

Recorded redemptive history starts with a man who was afflicted in order that he might raise up a godly generation; similarly, redemptive history will end with a generation of leaders who will come into apostleship through affliction. These apostles will be equipped to raise up a godly generation that will usher in Christ's second coming.

There is a generation that will be on the earth when Christ returns, and it will be a passionate generation that is pressing into its spiritual inheritance with violence (Matthew 11:12) and tenacity. Jesus is committed to preparing His bride and making her to be without spot or wrinkle, or any such thing, in preparation for His return. To get the kind of generation that will press into the kingdom with violent determination, God will visit the fathers. He will produce a Job generation that will be equipped to raise up the endtime bride of Christ.

"The first shall be last." The first Bible book ever written becomes the prototype for God's ways in the last hour.

It's very important that Job was not only afflicted, he was also healed. He was not only changed, he was given a testimony. Job had a personal experience with the resurrection power of God. Thus, demonstrations of resurrection power will attend the endtime apostles as "the signs of an apostle" (2 Corinthians 12:12) will once again be restored to the church.

God is going to restore incredible manifestations of power to His last days servants, but He will not do it without first taking them through the Job crucible. The pain of the Job crucible has great purpose. God can entrust the higher dimensions of kingdom authority only to those vessels that have been tempered, broken, and purified in the Job crucible. God will give His power only to safe vessels. He cannot entrust the power gifts to the unbroken. Those who know great victories without brokenness develop a triumphal spirit, and they are intolerable to live with. The endtime apostles will have been crushed first, so that the manifestations of power will be mingled with the perfume of humility, compassion, and desperate dependence.

The process will be painful, but the Job crucible will produce something glorious: servant leaders who have been entrusted with the authority to perform the greater works, in order to raise up an endtime generation that pursues its spiritual inheritance with violence. This is the bride for which Jesus is returning!

16

Job's Three Daughters

He also had seven sons and three daughters. And he called the name of the first Jemimah, the name of the second Keziah, and the name of the third Keren-Happuch. In all the land were found no women so beautiful as the daughters of Job; and their father gave them an inheritance among their brothers (42:13-15).

I asked this question: Why does the Bible give the names of Job's daughters, and not his sons? This is totally unparalleled in the Scriptures. Usually in Bible chronologies we are given the names of the sons, sometimes we get the names of both sons and daughters, but never are we given the daughters' names without the sons' names. This passage in Job is unique. What is its significance?

Here's the answer: Job's daughters represent the endtime bride. Job had been equipped to nurture and raise up the endtime bride of Christ.

In preparation for His return, Jesus is awakening His church to her bridal identity. The Scriptures use many metaphors and analogies to describe who we are collectively as the church. We are called a temple, a building, an army, a body, a bride, a brotherhood, a priesthood, a holy nation, a mountain, etc. Of all the images that help us understand who we are in Christ, the bridal image is the fullest and most sublime.

The last thing the Bible calls us is the bride— "And the Spirit and the bride say, 'Come!' (Revelation 22:17). Our endtime identity will be wrapped up, more than in any other representation, in our being the bride of Christ.

For the church to own her bridal identity, the Spirit of God has His work cut out for Him. Right now many in the church are more aware of our identity as an army or as a body. Those images are wonderful and instructive to us, but they are not the highest representation of our identity. It's true that Jesus is coming back for a body and for an army; but above all He's returning for His bride.

When Jesus looks at us, does He see an army? "Those are some mighty warriors; they're going to really help Me win this war!" Or does He see a body? "Love those kidneys, this body of Mine really works great for Me." No, when Jesus looks upon us He sees a bride for which He longs passionately. "You are My love, My darling, My betrothed; you are absolutely stunning in My eyes! I can't wait until we're together in the full consummation of the Father's plan!"

It's important that we come to see ourselves as a bride first and a worker second. This is the proper order of the two great commandments. *If we function as a warrior who loves, we will burn out from ministry exhaustion; but if we awaken to our identity as a bride who wars, we will discover true fulfillment and destiny.* Those who function as a worker who occasionally loves will eventually be depleted; those who give themselves first to bridal affections for the Lord Jesus, and then go to work from a pure love motive, will be able to constantly draw upon the inner resource of that abiding love relationship. No matter how hot the warfare gets, they will have grace to persevere.

A Shared Inheritance

"And their father gave them an inheritance among their brothers" (42:15). This verse is saying that the endtime bride will release the sisters to gain their full inheritance along with the brothers. This verse is hinting that before Jesus comes back, the church is finally going to get this thing right.

I'm talking about the "women in ministry" issue. I have wrestled with the scriptural witness to the unique function of women in ministry, as have most of us. I have agonized with many others over the Greek words that are used and their meaning. I personally don't feel that I have any answers for the dilemmas that attend this subject. But this verse suggests that God is going to give us a fuller understanding, which in my opinion is not yet manifest.

All of us have ached over the fact that in the midst of the dilemmas surrounding this issue, many of the sisters in the body of Christ have missed, forfeited, been denied, gone without, or lost their inheritance. That's going to change. I have no idea what this will look like, but we're going to get it right before it's all over.

And it will not be the daughters asserting themselves, demanding their inheritance. Nor will it be the brothers giving the inheritance to the sisters. Rather, it will be the fathers releasing the shared inheritance to the daughters. *God will so change the endtime fathers in the Job crucible that they will have the authority and wisdom to release the daughters into their inheritance.* When the fathers give the inheritance to the daughters, the brothers cannot object. The fathers have the right to distribute the inheritance as they see fit.

Although the daughters will not demand their inheritance, it's fitting that they ask for an inheritance. Let the spirit of Achsah, Caleb's daughter, come upon the endtime daughters. Achsah asked her father for a greater inheritance. Basically Achsah said, "Hey! Why should I have to settle for the flimsy inheritance of my husband simply because I'm a woman? My father is Caleb! God has given my father an awesome inheritance! And I want some of it!" So she incited her husband Othniel to ask Caleb for some land, which he gave him. But she still wasn't satisfied; she herself returned to Caleb and asked for springs of water. She wanted a water source for the land she had inherited. She approached her father very respectfully, which is shown by her dismounting from her donkey in order to speak with her father (Joshua 15:18); she was not brash or disrespectful. But her heart burned for her father's inheritance. And Caleb, in the generosity of his spirit, gave her a double portion—both the upper springs and the lower springs. "You have not because you ask not."

Jemimah

The names of Job's daughters are highly significant. In ancient times, names were assigned to children according to their personality or character qualities. Thus, the names of Job's three daughters are descriptive of the qualities of the endtime bride. By looking at the meanings of their names, we will see the three outstanding qualities of the endtime bride of Christ.

There is some variation between sources as to the meaning of Jemimah's name. One source points to two possible meanings: "a dove" or dovelike; and it also includes the idea of "day."[1] So Moffatt translates it "Ringdove." The Vulgate renders it "Day." Clarke's Commentary translates it "days upon days," adding this quote from the Chaldee text: "He called the first Jemimah, because she was as fair as the day."[2]

The most commonly agreed meaning of Jemimah is, "As Fair As The Day." Clarke's inflection of "days upon days" is also relevant, for I want to suggest that the meaning of Jemimah's name points to *the maturity of the endtime bride.*

---

[1] The Preacher's Homiletic Commentary, Volume 10. p. 281.
[2] Clarke's Commentary, Volume III, p. 193.

Jemimah represents the bride of Christ in her full maturity, prepared and made ready for her wedding day. She is getting married to the King of kings, and He deserves a bride that is mature and grown up in every way.

Imagine a man, on his wedding day, taking his bride to their hotel suite. As she opens her suitcase, she pulls out her barbie dolls and begins to set them up for play. Imagine the man's distress! He didn't know what he married! He thought he was marrying a woman of his own maturity level, and here she is on his wedding night, pulling out her childhood dolls.

Jesus does not want this kind of thing to happen to Him. He wants to marry a bride who thinks like Him, who talks on His wavelength, who shares His values and dreams, who is able to share in an eye-to-eye relationship. He wants and deserves a mature bride.

The passion of Ephesians 4:13-15 is that Christ's bride "come to the unity of the faith and of the knowledge of the Son of God, to a perfect man, to the measure of the stature of the fullness of Christ; that we should no longer be children, tossed to and fro and carried about with every wind of doctrine, by the trickery of men, in the cunning craftiness of deceitful plotting, but, speaking the truth in love, may grow up in all things into Him who is the head—Christ."

When the Scriptures describe the bride that Jesus will marry, they describe a bride of incredible maturity and readiness. When we look at the church today, she seems to be so immature and ill-prepared. So what is God going to do to prepare the bride for His Son?

The answer, I believe, is found in the context of the above quote, the context being: "And He Himself gave some to be apostles, some prophets, some evangelists, and some pastors and teachers, for the equipping of the saints for the work of ministry, for the edifying of the body of Christ" (Ephesians 4:11-12). *Here's how God is going to prepare the bride: He is going to take His five-fold ministries through the Job wilderness.*

When God's apostles, prophets, evangelists, pastors, and teachers will have come through the Job crucible, they will be supernaturally enabled to equip and prepare the endtime bride. There will have been such an acceleration of grace in their own lives that they will be vessels the Lord can use to accelerate the bride into a matured readiness for Christ's return.

Jemimah represents the loveliness of this endtime bride to Christ. As He beholds her, He is astounded and captivated. He says, "Father, You promised me a bride that I could relate to, a bride that would connect with Me on My maturity level. And now I see her! She is beautiful, Father! Thank you!"

Keziah

There is no discrepancy whatsoever among Hebrew language scholars as to the meaning of Keziah's name. They all agree; Keziah is the Cassia flower. Cassia is a beautiful fragrance that is mentioned a few places in the Bible.

There is one psalm that is the Book of Psalms' counterpart to the Song of Solomon—Psalm 45. Like the Song of Solomon, it deals with the marriage of the bride to the King. Psalm 45 mentions cassia in describing the King: "All Your garments are scented with myrrh and aloes and cassia" (Psalm 45:8).

Myrrh and aloes were commonly used as burial spices, and are specifically named as used for our Lord Jesus at His death (John 19:39). Therefore, Psalm 45:8 is referring to Christ's death. Cassia was one of the fragrances that denoted Christ's total consecration to the Father's purposes, even unto death. Thus, Keziah (or cassia) is a reference to *the endtime bride's consecration.* Her life is so totally submitted to the Kingdom and to God's will that she does not love her life to the death (Revelation 12:11). She holds no reservation in her heart about doing His will. Martyrdom is an honor, a privilege, a promotion. So she abandons herself to obeying the voice of her Lord, no matter what the cost.

This was the great cry of the apostle Paul:

Yet indeed I also count all things loss for the excellence of the knowledge of Christ Jesus my Lord, for whom I have suffered the loss of all things, and count them as rubbish, that I may gain Christ and be found in Him, not having my own righteousness, which is from the law, but that which is through faith in Christ, the righteousness which is from God by faith; that I may know Him and the power of His resurrection, and the fellowship of His sufferings, being conformed to His death, if, by any means, I may attain to the resurrection from the dead (Philippians 3:8-11).

This bride is so abandoned to God's purposes that not only is she *willing* to embrace death, she even *longs* to be "conformed to His death," that she might share in the passionate delight of knowing her Lover. This is pointing to the many martyrs who will lay their lives down to the death as a fragrance to God in the very last of the last days. Martyrdom is now on the increase worldwide, but it will flower even more as the return of Christ approaches.

But there's no self-pity with this bride. She has been totally resolved to the fact that she is called to be a fragrance among those who are perishing (2 Corinthians 2:15), and if that means being poured out as a drink offering for the faith of others (Philippians 2:17), she does not hesitate. She is totally His.

Keren-Happuch

The meaning of Keren-Happuch is much more difficult to construe than the names of her two sisters. There are two words here. Let's begin by looking at "Keren."

"Keren" has two equally valid meanings: "horn" or "ray." Which meaning is intended can be determined only by context. Interestingly, the context doesn't help us in this case. Most commentators are inclined toward the meaning of "horn," but others insist upon "ray." Personally, I think both meanings can have value and relevance.

Keren's meaning as "horn" can also be taken in a couple different ways. First of all, the term "horn" was used in military parlance to mean "power" or "strength." So one could see warfare language in Keren-Happuch's name. Or, "horn" was more commonly used to refer to a vial or a hollowed-out container. Or, some have connected it with a cornucopia—"a horn of plenty." Thus, one could see the imagery of abundance.

"Keren" can also be translated "ray." It is this meaning which is doubtless intended in Exodus 34:29-30 when it says "the skin of Moses' face shone." Rays of light actually burst forth from Moses' face. What glory! And what a beautiful image of the light that emanates from the endtime bride!

Now to the meaning of the second word in her name, "Happuch." The technical word for Happuch is "stibium," an ancient paint made originally from seaweed and later from antimony. This paint was used by oriental women around their eyes, as in the case of Jezebel (2 Kings 9:30). This eye paint was thought to make a woman's eyes large, shiny, and beautiful. It was applied to the eyelashes, eyelids, and eyebrows, making the eyelashes appear long and dark, and accentuating the sparkle of the eyes.[3]

"Happuch" has yet another interesting Bible usage. It is translated as "colorful gems" in the New King James Version of Isaiah 54:11: "O you afflicted one, tossed with tempest, and not comforted, behold, I will lay your stones with *colorful gems*, and lay your foundations with sapphires." In this reference the word actually refers to the *cement* that

---

[3] Barnes, Albert. Barnes' Notes, Job, pp. 275-276.

was used to adhere the stones to each other. It was a colored, highly ornamental cement that was used to enhance the beauty of a structure.

Therefore, in putting "Keren" and "Happuch" together, we encounter an interesting variety of opinions among scholars as to the correct meaning of her name. Perhaps most common is "Horn of Antimony" (so the Vulgate) or "Horn of Stibium" (Barnes' Notes). Using that line of translation, a more modern version might read "Vial of Mascara."

Clarke's Commentary calls it "the inverted or flowing horn, cornucopia, the horn of plenty."[4] Moffatt called her "Applescent." The Chaldee text says, "He called...the third Keren-happuch, because her face was as splendid as the emerald." The Preacher's Homiletic Commentary goes with either "the Horn of Paint" or "the Inverted Horn."[5] Fount Shults favors "Ray of Beauty."

It seems unlikely that we'll ever come up with one definitive meaning for her name. But the imagery of the various meanings is consistent: there is beauty enhancement, light, radiance, and sparkling eyes in her name.

Therefore, I am suggesting that Keren-Happuch's name points to the glory of the endtime bride. This bride is radiant with beauty, and she has a fire in her eyes for only One—her beloved Bridegroom, the Lord Jesus. There is a glory emanating from her life that cannot be denied, even by her enemies.

"That He might present her to Himself a glorious church, not having spot or wrinkle or any such thing, but that she should be holy and without blemish" (Ephesians 5:27). She will radiate a glory that even the world will recognize!

Before it's over, God will remove the church's reproach. We've been called "irrelevant," "prudish," and "powerless." But Jesus is going to fulfill the prophetic word, "I will no

---

[4] Clarke's Commentary, Volume III, p. 193.
[5] The Preacher's Homiletic Commentary, Volume 10. p. 282.

longer make you a reproach among the nations" (Joel 2:19). The bride of Christ will be glorious before all of heaven and earth.

The endtime bride will be fully mature (Jemimah). She will be a fragrance of consecration even unto death (Keziah). And she will be visibly glorious, radiant with beauty (Keren-Happuch).

Lord, raise up a Job generation that will be empowered to equip this kind of endtime bride!

17

Job's Attainments

Job came through the valley and attained some wonderful mountaintop blessings. Often we want the Job mountaintop without the Job crucible. We want what Job attained but don't want the pilgrimage to that attainment. But there are many today who are being given an insatiable hunger for the higher things. They're blessed; they're happy; they're overflowing, but yet somehow empty. They're not satisfied. They know there's got to be more. They want Job's revelation of God. And they're willing to pay the price.

In this chapter we will summarize the glorious things Job attained because he remained faithful to God in the greatest crisis of his life.

Wealth And Honor

First, but of the least significance, Job was restored to even greater wealth and honor and influence. In fact, Job is rewarded in the end with a double blessing. Compare his possessions at the beginning of the book with those at the end of the book:

- **Also, his possessions were seven thousand sheep, three thousand camels, five hundred yoke of oxen, five hundred female donkeys,**

> **and a very large household, so that this man was the greatest of all the people of the East** (1:3).
> - **Now the LORD blessed the latter days of Job more than his beginning; for he had fourteen thousand sheep, six thousand camels, one thousand yoke of oxen, and one thousand female donkeys** (42:12).

Simple arithmetic computes that Job's possessions after his deliverance were double of that which he had before his calamity. This is consistent with the testimony of Scripture: "Instead of your shame you shall have double honor, and instead of confusion they shall rejoice in their portion. Therefore in their land they shall possess double; everlasting joy shall be theirs" (Isaiah 61:7).

Look at this compelling passage: "As for you also, because of the blood of your covenant, I will set your prisoners free from the waterless pit. Return to the stronghold, you prisoners of hope. Even today I declare that I will restore double to you" (Zechariah 9:11-12). The Lord speaks a double restoration to the exiles of Zion who were prisoners of hope in Babylon. Although imprisoned in a foreign land, they carried a hope of God's promised return to the stronghold of Zion. Because they kept their hearts pure in this hope (1 John 3:3), the Lord assured them they would emerge from their prison with a double portion. The literal rendering of Job 42:10 is, **"The Lord turned the captivity of Job when he prayed for his friends."** So Job's ordeal is called a prison. When Job was delivered from his prison the Lord poured a double blessing on his life.

There was a restoration of Job's social life, which is described in Job 42:11— **"Then all his brothers, all his sisters, and all those who had been his acquaintances before, came to him and ate food with him in his house."** After his months of dark solitude, Job once again became sought out and his time came into demand. (Note: If you're bored in prison, store up on your rest; once delivered, you will be busier than ever.)

Through God's blessings, Job was reinstated to his former place of honor among his contemporaries and was promoted to an even greater place of influence than before. God vindicated His servant who was faithful to Him.

Character Change

Secondly, Job was profoundly changed in his character and personhood. The wilderness changed the way he thought; it changed his values, his perspective on the kingdom of God, how he viewed life.

Job came through as a giant of the faith. "That the genuineness of your faith, being much more precious than gold that perishes, though it is tested by fire, may be found to praise, honor, and glory at the revelation of Jesus Christ" (1 Peter 1:7). When our faith comes through the fire, it becomes very precious—to God. When God sees a faith that believes Him even when everything is black, this kind of faith touches His heart like nothing else. It's so beautiful to Him that He's committed to enhancing it. *When God finds a Job who will trust Him in the face of overwhelmingly contrary circumstances, God's heart is moved beyond measure.* So God brought Job through with a totally refined faith. **"When He has tested me, I shall come forth as gold"** (23:10).

The wilderness also changed the way he fathered. His first set of children forfeited their inheritance because of "spiritual passivity," but Job was so changed by the crucible that he was able to raise his second set of children in such a way that they became a generation that was spiritually proactive and aggressive—with a passion for their inheritance.

This speaks prophetically of the last hour. *God will be taking His servants through the Job crucible that they might be equipped to raise up an endtime generation that will pursue their spiritual inheritance with kingdom violence* (Matthew 11:12). Virtually every generation has been offered

the endtime inheritance, but through passivity each generation continues to say no, even to this present hour. But
there is a generation that will say yes, and they will be
prepared for that greater consecration by fathers who have
been changed in the crucible.

Job's character changes are evidenced in his final words
in the book:

> **Then Job answered the LORD and said: "I know
> that You can do everything, and that no purpose
> of Yours can be withheld from You. You asked,
> 'Who is this who hides counsel without knowl-
> edge?' Therefore I have uttered what I did not un-
> derstand, things too wonderful for me, which I did
> not know. Listen, please, and let me speak; You
> said, 'I will question you, and you shall answer
> Me.' I have heard of You by the hearing of the ear,
> but now my eye sees You. Therefore I abhor my-
> self, and repent in dust and ashes"** (42:1-6).

"I know that You can do everything"—Job's faith was
stronger and purer than ever. He came away with a great
confidence in God's sovereign power! It was of this puri-
fying of our faith that Peter spoke when he wrote, "that
the genuineness of your faith, being much more precious
than gold that perishes, though it is tested by fire, may be
found to praise, honor, and glory at the revelation of Jesus
Christ" (1 Peter 1:7). The endtime apostles will move in
extraordinary demonstrations of faith, but it will be a faith
that has been tested severely and been proven true in the
crucible. They will suffer great affliction, be changed in the
process, and also be delivered through God's power, qualifying them to administer that same grace to others.

**"And that no purpose of Yours can be withheld from
You"**—This verse articulates a great tension between the
faith that moves God's hand and the understanding that
God acts sovereignly in accordance with His purposes. The

endtime apostles will not only move in great demonstrations of faith, but they will also own a great awareness that God operates through divine purpose. When God decides to do something, nothing can stop His purpose; and when He purposes to withhold something, no amount of faith posturing can change His mind. *The highest dimensions of faith will be entrusted to those who have learned to partner with God in fulfilling His purposes in the earth* (as opposed to fulfilling their own ministry-building agenda).

"I have uttered what I did not understand, things too wonderful for me, which I did not know"—Job came away from the crucible with a profound appreciation for his own finiteness, his limitations, his nothingness without God. Although he was refined as a vessel useful for noble purposes in God's house (2 Timothy 2:21), he had been so broken in the Potter's hands that he carried the marks of that brokenness with him to the most noble of entrustments.

Healing

Of Job's mountaintop attainments, thirdly, he was healed. **"The Lord turned the captivity of Job when he prayed for his friends"** (42:10, margin). Job didn't simply transition into a better lifestyle; God sovereignly visited him and healed him. Job experienced the miraculous, supernatural power of God.

Job's healing is absolutely critical to the book's message and a vital ingredient for understanding how the book speaks to the endtime generation. Here's why his healing is so crucial: Job was given a testimony for the next generation.

It is imperative that the young ones see the resurrection power of God in their generation. We can talk about how God healed our grandmother, or about what God did back in 1965. And the story may be rich, but it's not good enough for this 21st century generation. They have got to see God's power for themselves.

This was one of the critical elements that distinguished Job's second set of children from his first children. His second set of children were witnesses of God's power; they had a testimony of God's visitation to their father, something Job's first ten children didn't have. They were first-hand participants in the reality that God delivers the righteous. God's demonstrated resurrection power burned something into Job's second set of children that empowered them to rise up to true greatness and spiritual beauty.

Please let me share a personal story with you, which will communicate why this truth is so important to me. When I was thirteen years old, my mother became ill with tumors in her breasts. We suspected cancer although she felt specifically directed of the Lord not to get a biopsy. Her health plummeted rapidly. Soon she was virtually bedridden, incapable of many normal daily functions such as meal preparation.

I watched my parents begin to pursue God with a heretofore unparalleled desperation. I would leave for school in the morning with my mother sitting on the couch, reading the Word. I would come home from school to find my mother kneeling at the couch, kleenex nearby, crying out to God. My father (a pastor) was also going to his office and crying out to God in a similar way. Their pursuit of God became a full-time, 24-hour passion. They were desperate for a breakthrough because without it my mother was dying.

The story is fascinating and sublime (I tell it in more detail in my book, *The Fire Of Delayed Answers*), but here's the bottom line: my mother was healed instantaneously one evening while my parents were worshiping God. At the time of this writing, she has just turned 70 years old, and is filled with strength and vigor!

But here's the thing that was burned into the heart of this 13-year-old as I watched God answer my parents: *Seek God with all your heart, and He will be found of you.* I own a personal conviction that the answer to every problem is found in a hot pursuit of the face of Christ. This truth was burned into me as I witnessed the supernatural healing power of God touch my mother.

And now, many years later, as I am personally facing the greatest crisis of my life, I have been equipped through my parents' testimony with a passion for seeking God with everything I've got. And here's what I'm contending for: I'm believing that God will visit me and heal me with His resurrection power, that my children might witness the supernatural power of God touching their father, because I've got three worldchangers in my home! I believe that my kids are going to be leaders in their generation, equipped for mighty exploits in God's grace. When they see the power of God touch me, it will burn something into their hearts that no heat or pressure or crisis will ever be able to strip from them.

As the first Bible book written, the book of Job speaks to the last day. Job is a type of the endtime apostles. Job's healing speaks of the remarkable apostolic power that will be released in the last hour. The last-days apostles who are used in the highest dimensions of the miraculous will also be those who suffer the most. *God will entrust the highest dimensions of power only to those who have been chastened with suffering, for they are safe vessels.* Paul exercised such unusual power and authority because he had suffered so much. Only those who suffer in the flesh are kept pure from the arrogating, self-vaunting proclivities of the flesh.

A Revelation Of God

Finally, Job was given a front-seat, first-hand revelation of God! Nothing changed Job more than this paradigm-revolutionizing encounter with God.

There is nothing greater to covet. Moses cried, "Lord, show me Your glory." He wanted to see God! Let this longing flood your heart, a passion for God to open your eyes and reveal His beauty.

When God chooses to meet with us, He doesn't condescend and stoop to our level. He lifts us up to His level! God doesn't come down to Job, he lifts Job up to His throne. This is the glory and splendor for which Job had panted back in 19:27!

Job's last words make the hungry salivate: **"I have heard of You by the hearing of the ear, but now my eye sees You. Therefore I abhor myself, and repent in dust and ashes"** (42:6). This first-person encounter with God baptized Job into a passionately intimate relationship with God. Now Job knew God in a dimension of intimacy based upon shared experience. (Note: The promotion of the Lord is not necessarily a higher position in the echelons of men, although it can include that. But even better, it is a lifting up to higher spiritual realities. It is the higher place of fuller intimacy, greater revelation, of unhindered knowing.)

Job entered into the promise Jesus left us, "Blessed are the pure in heart, for they shall see God" (Matthew 5:8). Job had kept himself pure, even in his distress, and he was rewarded with the greatest gift any man can possibly receive in this life: a vision of God.

Job had come to know Him who is from the beginning, the foremost quality of spiritual fathers—"I write to you, fathers, because you have known Him who is from the beginning" (1 John 2:13). It takes a powerful revelation of God to launch someone into this dimension of spiritual fatherhood.

"Therefore I abhor myself, and repent in dust and ashes." Someone might say, "See! The issue in Job's life really was repentance! If he had repented at the beginning of the book, he wouldn't have had to go through all that." No, my friend, you don't get it.

Job is having the same experience here as Isaiah, who when he saw God said, "Woe is me, for I am undone! Because I am a man of unclean lips, and I dwell in the midst of a people of unclean lips; for my eyes have seen the King, the LORD of hosts' (Isaiah 6:5). This is the experience of

Daniel who, when he saw God, was ill for several days. This is the experience of Ezekiel who fell on his face before the glory of the Lord. This is the experience of the apostle John who, when he saw his friend with whom he had lived for three years, fell to the ground like a dead man because of the supreme glory of the resurrected Christ.

Job was seeing God in His pristine splendor, and his only response could be that of deprecating himself and glorifying God. He saw how bankrupt he really was in contrast to the riches of the glory of God. But oh, what wonder and magnificence he beheld! *Even though God's self-revelation may be difficult for we humans to process, the surpassing greatness of beholding Him is worth it!*

Now, this was not simply a one-time act of repentance on Job's part. He wasn't simply saying, "I'm sorry, Lord, for my brash words and bad attitudes." Job was saying that he had come away from his trial with a profound awareness of his own weakness, inadequacy, insignificance, emptiness, and absolute nothingness apart from God. He was a broken man. *This sense of personal bankruptcy would never leave him because it was purchased in the fire, and it would enable him to walk in true dependence and humility before the Lord for the rest of his life.*

Part of Job's revelation of God included things that chapters 38-42 don't detail. Actually, aspects of that revelation are detailed in chapters 1-2. At some point in time after Job's release, he was granted a revelation into the throneroom of God. Job experienced something similar to the apostle Paul, who wrote of himself, "I know a man in Christ who fourteen years ago—whether in the body I do not know, or whether out of the body I do not know, God knows—such a one was caught up to the third heaven. And I know such a man—whether in the body or out of the body I do not know, God knows—how he was caught up into Paradise and heard inexpressible words, which it is not lawful for a man to utter" (2 Corinthians 12:2-4). In the end, God revealed to Job how the heavenly drama unfolded that launched his entire ordeal. Job saw the throne, and he was shown the manner in which the holy **"sons of God came to present themselves before the Lord"** (1:6).

I believe it's safe to suggest that Job was the first human being to be granted a glimpse (from earth) of God's glorious throne. He was given insight into heavenly realities. He also revelled in the incredible affection that God poured on him when God showed him what He thought about him all along. "You felt like that about me from the start??" Job must have wondered. This is God saying to Job, "You are fair, my love; you have dove's eyes; you are the only one of your mother."

This revelation of God revolutionized Job's priorities in the kingdom. God had turned him from "a worker who loves" into "a lover who works." This motivational shift is on top of the Holy Spirit's agenda for this hour. He is revealing Himself to us so that we might grow out of our servant model and enter into a bridal awareness. The overriding paradigm being modelled in the church today is that of the servant, the worker who loves. Almost every conference is focused on raising up workers. But God is changing this. *The revelation of Christ as our Bridegroom will awaken us to our identity first and foremost as lovers of God.* The flame of that passion will in turn ignite the greatest labors for the kingdom, with no burnout, because nothing equips us for persevering service better than lovesickness.

For those who are waiting for a revelation of God, let me give one last encouragement: "With the merciful You will show Yourself merciful; with a blameless man You will show Yourself blameless; with the pure You will show Yourself pure" (Psalm 18:25-26). The merciful, blameless, pure man holds this confidence: "You *will* show Yourself." Yes!

Scaling The Mountain

Psalm 18 parallels Job 42, because it's the psalm of answered prayer. In Psalm 18, David rejoices in the victory God has given him over all his enemies. As he exults in

God's deliverance, David talks about how the Lord brought him out into a broad, high place. He writes, "He makes my feet like the feet of deer, and sets me on my high places" (Psalm 18:33).

Like Job, David is saying, "God not only answered my prayer; He lifted me to a higher place than I had ever known." Job was elevated to the high places of the Spirit, and he enjoyed the delights of God that are attained at the mountaintop of answered prayer.

But as I meditated in Psalm 18:33, I saw this: *the highlands of spiritual promotion are treacherously steep.* The highest heights in God are not rounded hills, they are jutting escarpments. The high places of the Spirit are characterized by sheer cliffs and steep embankments. In order to navigate that kind of rocky terrain, we must first have our feet trained like that of a deer.

I have talked to deer hunters, and they speak with amazement and awe about the ability of deer to navigate steep inclines. A deer's foot is not hard like the hoof of a horse, but it is softer and more supple. Therefore, its hooves function almost like fingers, and a deer will appear to almost grab onto the rock as it climbs the side of a mountain. It is able to gain a foothold on the most meager slices of outcropping rock formations. Deer are able to navigate steep slopes, bounding upward with incredible speed and awe-inspiring grace.

The high places of God are treacherously hazardous. If you take a fall on the lower hills of God, you might sustain some cuts and bruises, but then you can pick yourself up, brush yourself off, and move onward. Not so on the higher elevations. If you take a fall on the higher precipices of God's high places, it can mean your destruction.

Church history is laden with stories of men and women who took a fall on the higher things of the Spirit. Some of these hazards are: spiritual pride, elitism, judgmentalism, a religious spirit, an independent spirit, self-deception, feelings of being indispensable, dealing with the praise of man when you are granted higher revelation, properly steward-ing the influence over people that comes when others hon-or your attainments, handling the finances that flow with the anointing...and the list goes on. These hazards have the potential to destroy if not navigated properly.

Spiritual fathers are able to guide the younger believ-ers as they climb the mountain of God because they paid the price to discover the pitfalls. *Spiritual fathers are those who have the scars to prove they've already traversed the dangerous paths of the high road in God.* They've scraped their knees on the jagged hazards, and they're able to say, "Don't step there!"

God has higher things for you; He designs to bring you into the high things of the Spirit. But He loves you too much to give you the mountain without the training of your feet. So He'll take you into the valley, where He brings you into the intense training of your feet. Then, when you begin to walk the mountains of God, you will walk that terrain with extreme caution, humility, brokenness, and implicit dependence upon God.

The Scriptures give us a stunning example of a man who walked the high places of God, and took a fall to his destruc-tion. The man I'm referring to was the son of the writer of Psalm 18:33. When David gave the kingdom of Israel to his son Solomon, everything was in place. The nation was pros-perous, they had peace on every border, and true worship was established in the sanctuary. Solomon was handed the kingdom on a silver platter. He got it all—with ease.

Then, the smartest man who ever lived did the dumbest thing. Solomon—the man to whom God had supernatural-ly given incredible wisdom and brainpower—worshiped a block of wood. Think of it! He worshiped an inanimate idol! (His many wives seduced him into idolatry.) We're talking about a man who wrote entire books of the Bible! Solomon had walked the highlands of the Song of Solomon and be-held the hidden treasures of Proverbs. And now he wor-ships an idol? What is wrong with this picture?

It's true that Solomon attained marvelous heights in the Spirit, but he didn't have his feet trained as a deer in the valley. He got everything too easily. Unlike his father David, who spent seven years running as a fugitive for his life from king Saul, Solomon had no wilderness years. He had no crucible. He got the promotion without the pruning. He scaled the mountain without first plummeting into the valley, and as a result he was not sufficiently prepared for the treacherous precipices of the mountain.

The Lord loves you too much to allow you to self-destruct on the high places, as did Solomon. Therefore, He trains your feet in the Job valley, sensitizing your walk to the hazards, and equipping you to navigate the heights of God with grace and beauty.

God doesn't impose the Job crucible on anyone. He grants it to those with an insatiable cry in their hearts for the higher inheritance. Do not fear, God will not lead you in a path for which you do not desperately plead. And if He brings you into the Job crucible, do not fear—it's because of His great affection for you (Revelation 3:19).

Make no mistake, the heights of God carry a great price-etag. Let the wise count the cost. But look at what Job attained! And take it from someone who is climbing the mountain: *it's worth it!!*

But as it is written: **"Eye has not seen, nor ear heard, nor have entered into the heart of man the things which God has prepared for those who love Him"** (1 Corinthians 2:9).

Description of Resources Available on the Facing Page

❖ ENVY: THE ENEMY WITHIN — This short but gripping book reveals how ambitious motives and carnal comparisons between ministries can hinder the release of God's blessings. Explore how 2-talent saints envy 5-talent saints. Riveting, provocative, and controversial.

❖ SECRETS OF THE SECRET PLACE—Bob shares some of the secrets he's learned in making the secret place energizing and delightful. Gain fresh fuel for your secret devotional life with God!

❖ GLORY: WHEN HEAVEN INVADES EARTH is Bob's most recent book on worship — for worshipers with a passion to see God. May your vision be renewed and clarified for a personal, life-changing encounter with God Himself.

❖ DEALING WITH THE REJECTION AND PRAISE OF MAN is a booklet that shows how to hold your heart before God in a way that pleases Him in the midst of both rejection and praise from people.

❖ THE FIRE OF DELAYED ANSWERS explores how God sometimes delays the answers to our prayers in order to produce godly character in us. This book is "spiritual food" for those in crisis or difficulty.

❖ THE FIRE OF GOD'S LOVE compels us toward the passionate love that God is producing within the bride in this hour for her Bridegroom, the Lord Jesus.

❖ IN HIS FACE propels the reader passionately toward a more personal and intimate relationship with Jesus Christ. Challenging devotional reading.

❖ EXPLORING WORSHIP is a 300-page textbook that covers a full range of subjects related to praise and worship. Translated into several languages, this bestselling book is being used internationally as a text by many Bible colleges, Bible study groups, and worship leading teams.

All of Bob Sorge's Titles

PAIN, PERPLEXITY, AND PROMOTION:
A Prophetic Interpretation of the Book of Job $14
A COVENANT WITH MY EYES $13
EXPLORING WORSHIP:
A Practical Guide to Praise & Worship $16
Exploring Worship WORKBOOK & DISCUSSION GUIDE .... $ 5
IN HIS FACE: A Prophetic Call to Renewed Focus $13
THE FIRE OF DELAYED ANSWERS $14
THE FIRE OF GOD'S LOVE $13
DEALING WITH THE REJECTION AND PRAISE OF MAN $10
GLORY: When Heaven Invades Earth $10
SECRETS OF THE SECRET PLACE $15
Secrets of the Secret Place: COMPANION STUDY GUIDE $11
Secrets of the Secret Place: LEADER'S MANUAL .... $ 5
ENVY: The Enemy Within $12
FOLLOWING THE RIVER: A Vision for Corporate Worship $10
LOYALTY: The Reach of the Noble Heart $14
UNRELENTING PRAYER $13
POWER OF THE BLOOD: Approaching God with Confidence $13
IT'S NOT BUSINESS, IT'S PERSONAL $10
OPENED FROM THE INSIDE: Taking the Stronghold of Zion $11
MINUTE MEDITATIONS $12
BETWEEN THE LINES: God is Writing Your Story $13

DVD Series:
EXPLORING WORSHIP DVD SERIES $30
SECRETS OF THE SECRET PLACE DVD SERIES $30

To order Bob's materials:
- Go to www.oasishouse.com
- Call 816-767-8880 (ask about quantity discounts)
- Write Oasis House, PO Box 522, Grandview, MO 64030-0522

Go to www.oasishouse.com for special package discounts, book descriptions, ebooks, and free teachings.